WHAT THE CATHOLIC FAITHFUL CAN DO

Gerard Morrissey

CHRISTENDOM COLLEGE PRESS
Route 3, Box 87
Front Royal, Virginia 22630

ISBN Number: 0-931888-23-9

CONTENTS

Introduction

This is the third and last book in which we consider what each of us can do to defend the Holy Father and to promote the Church's teaching. In the first book our goal was to know what the Church's teaching is—at least on some of the crucial points currently being disputed by Church dissenters. In the second book our goal was to understand the present situation—how the problem arose. Now, in this third book, we ask what we can do about it.

At the outset let me say that I do not have all of the answers. I will suggest certain ideas but I hope that each of you will reflect on the ideas presented and then add your own thoughts. I can only take you a part of the way but I hope it will help many Catholics to realize how important their involvement is to defend the Church's teaching.

Let us begin by imagining that you are a Catholic of no special position or influence within the Church. Perhaps you are the mother or father of four or five children. You want to bring your children up so that they love the Catholic religion the way that you loved it. As you consider it, there are really three things that you would like to do: a) to deepen your own faith, b) to pass on this faith to your children, and c) to work within your own parish (and within the Church community at large) in defense of the Pope and the Church's official teaching. How to do each of these three things will be the subject of this book.

1.
Yes You Can

As we consider the task before us—to promote the Church's teaching in our own families and in the entire Church community—let us first face a question that will probably come immediately into our minds. Can we ourselves really do very much?

Yes, we can.

No matter what problems we have—no matter how limited our opportunities at first sight might appear to be—each of us can be a tremendous force in promoting Christ's message. Perhaps you look at yourself and say: "How can I really do all this? I don't have any particular talents. In my view, I am not that intelligent. I do not even have a degree from college. I am not a gifted speaker. I am not somebody with great knowledge about the Church situation. I'm simply an ordinary layman or laywoman who is a committed Catholic."

Even if you seem to have no particular talents, God's Grace can accomplish wonders through you—provided that you work as hard as you can to cooperate. Certainly, particular talents are helpful. If you do have a special talent (e.g., intelligence, speaking ability, writing ability), this can be a great gift to the Church. However, even if you seem to have no particular talents at all, you can still be a modern apostle for the Church's teaching.

No matter how lacking in opportunity it may seem that you are, you are certainly in no worse a situation than were the Apostles themselves when Jesus chose them to carry on His Work. If we think about it, what a strange choice Our Lord made! At the time of Christ's Mission, the people with the talent and the education and the power were the Romans. Yet Jesus did not choose a person like Caesar Augustus—a man of almost unlimited power. No. Instead, Jesus chose a few unlettered Jewish fishermen and tax collectors—ordinary people from a very insignificant section of the Roman Empire.

Imagine how the Apostles must have felt at Pentecost. Here they were—lacking intellectual knowledge, lacking wealth, coming from a poor part of the world. They were up against the Roman Empire—

opposed by people who had far more talents, opportunity, and power than they did. How could they possibly succeed?

Through God's Grace, however, we know what happened. And, as we read Sacred Scripture, we see it happening again and again. Those called by God (e.g., Moses in the Old Testament) protest that they really do not have the talent or the ability to carry out the mission for which they have been summoned. God seems to go out of His Way to select people who do not have such abilities. As St. Paul reminds us in his first epistle to the Corinthians, God deliberately chooses the weak things of the world to confound the strong:

> Brothers you are among those called. Consider your own situation. Not many of you are wise as men account wisdom; not many are influential; and surely not many are well born. God chose those whom the world considers absurd to shame the wise; He singled out the weak of this world to shame the strong, He chose the world's low-born and despised, those who count for nothing to reduce to nothing those who were something; so that mankind can do no boasting before God. God it is who has given you life in Christ Jesus.

The reason all this is true is that— when we talk about promoting the Church's teaching—talents may be very important, but it is goodness that influences people above everything else, and it does not seem to matter whether it is goodness with talent or goodness without talent.

Think for a moment of the people who have had a special influence on you in your life. They are not necessarily the intelligent or the gifted, but those people who have been loving and generous.

I recall one couple who had a great influence on me by their charity towards others in the parish. Whenever an individual needed help, this couple was willing to open their own home and to give of themselves in a very special way. They were definitely not the most intelligent people in the parish, nor were they wealthy by any means. But they radiated a Christ-like goodness and it was this above all that enabled them to bring Jesus to others.

God has promised us only one thing . . . Himself. We are not promised the gifts of health, of long life, of intelligence, of the ability to speak, etc. Nevertheless, we have the most important thing of all—the promise that, if we so choose,—if we will—we will never be separated from God. And we have the further promise that, if we will allow God to work through us, His Grace will reach out in a special way to those for whom we pray and work.

Of course, if we are truly Christ-like, we will never know it. One of the ironies involved is that if we think we are good, we are probably close to pride. Nevertheless, even though we may always consider ourselves imperfect—even though we may never be fully like those saints who are our models—yet we can try. If we do, God can work marvels through us.

GIVING WITNESS TO CHURCH TEACHING

As we discussed in Book II, when we speak of reflecting Christ it is not simply a matter of feeling. There is an intellectual content to our faith. We believe that Jesus is truly God, that Jesus is literally present in the Eucharist, and so on. In other words, our lives must teach others the importance of both devotion and doctrine. We love, but our love is based on what we believe Jesus has truly done for us. These two elements—doctrine and devotion—must both be present. If we believe in what Christ has done, but then do not live this faith in our lives, then our belief is sterile. On the other hand, if someone says it does not really matter what the truth is so long as one is sincere—so long as one "feels" something—then one reduces religion to a matter of subjective emotion. The truth is that it does matter what Jesus has done. We believe that the teaching of the Church is literally true. Because we believe, we must then respond with love.

Now because religion does involve this intellectual or "doctrinal" aspect—because we must learn about and study the Church's teachings—many parents tend to think they are not capable of teaching religion to their children. Therefore, they delegate the teaching function to "experts" who they believe have the knowledge the parents themselves do not possess. As we discussed in our previous books, these experts often undermine the Church's teaching instead of reinforcing it.

Even with respect to the intellectual aspect of our religion, however, it is important for every parent to understand that learning Catholic doctrine is not nearly as difficult as one might assume at first glance. The basic teachings can be grasped rather easily although it is also true to say that we can spend the rest of our lives and never exhaust the depths of such teachings. However, it is certainly possible for all of us to know Catholic doctrine well enough both to appreciate it ourselves and to pass on this knowledge and appreciation to others. Some intellectuals complicate things tremendously. The truth is that the kind of "knowledge" intellectuals sometimes pretend is essential is not really needed at all.

I might add that this statement is true not only with respect to religion but in other areas as well. For example, suppose you wish to pass on to your children a love of literature—an appreciation of writers such as Shakespeare and Dickens. On the one hand, there is a role for the "expert" in studying Shakespeare and Dickens. On the other hand, all of us—not just the "experts"—can appreciate good literature.

So it is with our faith. On the one hand, there is certainly great value in the contributions of the true "experts" (as opposed to those "pseudo-experts" who substitute their own thinking for the teaching of the Church). On the other hand, our religion is not just for the person with fifty degrees but for all of us. It simply is not true that only the intelligent are "first-class" Christians—just as it is not true that only the academic professor can appreciate Dickens. In fact, whether we are talking about literature or religion, the person with a great amount of technical and academic knowledge does not necessarily appreciate the reality more than the "common man".

Sometimes the reason we can think it is beyond our capacity to teach doctrine to others is that we have never done it. Whenever we undertake something for the first time, it is only natural for us to consider it very complex. Recall how difficult it seemed to be when you first learned to swim or to drive a car or when you first tried to know the names of the various stars in the skies. Nevertheless, once you started off, were you not surprised at the progress you made? What appeared to be a tremendous obstacle at the beginning turned out to be much less so once you started the project and kept to it.

The same is true with teaching Catholic doctrine. Despite any fears you may have about your competence, if you will spend the time to study the Church's teaching (perhaps as little as fifteen minutes a day using a book by an orthodox Catholic theologian) you will be surprised at how quickly you will become knowledgeable enough and confident enough to pass on your knowledge and love of Catholic doctrine to your children and to others.

If you are a parent, please remember that nobody can match a mother and father in teaching Catholic doctrine to their children. The Catholic Church recognizes this important truth and that is the reason the Church strongly encourages parents to teach doctrine to their sons and daughters. To quote directly from the Second Vatican Council (*Lumen Gentium, 41*):

Christian married couples and parents, following their own way, should support one another in grace all through life with faithful love, and should train their children (lovingly received from God) in Christian doctrine and evangelical virtues. Because in this way they present to all an example of unfailing and generous love, they build up the brotherhood of charity, and they stand as witnesses and cooperators of the fruitfulness of Mother Church, as a sign of, and a share in that love with which Christ loved his bride and gave himself for her.

And to quote further from Pope John Paul II (in his 1979 document on religious education entitled "Catechesi Tradendae"):

The family's catechetical activity has a special character, which is in a sense irreplaceable. This special character has been rightly stressed by the Church, particularly by the Second Vatican Council. Education in the faith by parents, which should begin from the children's tenderest age, is already being given when the members of a family help each other to grow in faith through the witness of their Christian lives, a witness that is often without words but which perseveres throughout a day-to-day life lived in accordance with the Gospel. This catechesis is more incisive when, in the course of family events (such as the reception of the sacraments, the celebration of great liturgical feasts, the birth of a child, a bereavement) care is taken to explain in the home the Christian or religious content of these events. But that is not enough: Christian parents must strive to follow and repeat, within the setting of family life, the more methodical teaching received elsewhere. The fact that these truths about the main questions of faith and Christian living are thus repeated within a family setting impregnated with love and respect will often make it possible to influence the children in a decisive way of life. The parents themselves profit from the effort that this demands of them, for in a catechetical dialogue of this sort each individual both receives and gives.

Family catechesis therefore precedes, accompanies, and enriches all other forms of catechesis. Furthermore, in places where anti-religious legislation endeavours even to prevent education in the faith, and in places where widespread unbelief or invasive secularism makes real religious growth practically impossible, the Church of the home remains the one place where children and young people can receive an authentic catechesis. Thus there cannot be too great an effort on the part of Christian parents to prepare for this ministry of being their own children's catechists and to carry it out with tireless zeal.

THE QUESTION OF TIME

In this section we have been considering the person with no special background, but with a desire to do something—perhaps the parents of some young children, who want to deepen their own faith, and pass faith on to their children.

One obvious question comes to mind. Does a busy parent have the time to do this properly? Perhaps each parent has a job. They must struggle in their daily living. Do they really have the time to teach religion to their children?

It would certainly take a tremendous amount of time if one attempted to do everything the first day. But on the contrary, they are trying to teach religion to their children over many years.

Instead of time, the real problem we often face in such situations is disciplining ourselves to make the necessary effort every day. For instance, we may say that we do not have time to exercise. In truth, however, it is relatively easy to find the necessary fifteen minutes or half an hour a day to exercise. The hard part is to "force" ourselves to do it—to develop the will-power to carry out a program that we know is good for us.

As applied to religion, most parents can certainly find the time to learn enough about their religion so that they can become excellent teachers of their children. However, they may have to "discipline" themselves to do it. They may have to make a resolve—and keep to it—to put aside a certain amount of time each day to learn about the Catholic faith. If parents can do this—if they can give as little as fifteen minutes or half hour a day to this—it will mount up and they will soon find themselves able to speak out effectively on behalf of the Church's teaching.

One other thing can be said about this matter of time. If a parent were to say "I don't have the time to study Catholic doctrine and to teach it to my children because it is an all-out struggle for me to take care of my children's material needs", then that parent, even if he or she is very sincere, is making a serious mistake. After all, what good does it do if our children are fed and clothed but they lose the most important thing of all—their Catholic faith? In this regard we can recall the words of Our Lord to Martha and Mary. Martha was so busy with the practical matters of day-to-day living that she did not have the time (or so she thought) to listen to Jesus. Our Lord corrected her. He told Martha that listening to

Jesus was the single most important thing that she could do. This was not to deny the value of Martha's work, for in fact she was a saint. Nor was it to deny that Martha's day-to-day work most certainly had to be done. Our Lord was correcting her on one thing only, namely, her judgment that she (and her sister Mary) did not have the time to listen. As applied to us, the message of Jesus is that listening to the Word of God as it comes to us in the doctrines taught by Christ through His Church is more important than anything else in our life.

I doubt that the importance of Christian doctrine has to be emphasized to those reading this book. You would probably not be reading these words at present if you did not think doctrine was important. But some-times I have found that Church dissenters grab Martha's argument and use it against lay people who are attempting to promote orthodox Catholic teaching. The dissenters say: "You should be taking care of your family instead". The truth is that those lay people who speak up on behalf of the Church's teaching *are* taking care of God's family—not only their own children but all the other members of Christ's Church for whom they are laboring.

In summary, we do not have to choose between either the demands of day-to-day living or the important work of learning Church doctrine and speaking up for it. We can do both. In fact, the Church's mission will not be carried out properly unless all Catholics (clergy and lay, "expert" and "non-expert") attempt to carry out both functions as well as they can throughout their lives.

TWO QUALITIES THAT WE NEED

We said previously that special talents, while helpful, are not neces-sary to speak out effectively on behalf of Church doctrine.

But there are two general qualities that are definitely important. First, we need to love. Second, we need to persevere.

Earlier we considered the example of Moses and of the Apostles huddled together in the Upper Room after Our Lord's Ascension. Like us, they wondered how they could possibly succeed until they realized that God chooses the weak things of the world to confound the strong.

In promoting the Church's teaching, prayer is needed above every-thing else. We must pray to God for the strength to act as He wants us to act. We must also offer up our own sufferings for this intention. (In this regard it should be stressed that the sufferings of the sick and the dying can be invaluable if they are offered up for the purpose of promoting the Church's teaching.)

Throughout this book we will consider some of the problems that we may encounter in speaking up for Church doctrine. For example, we will almost certainly be attacked—sometimes even viciously. Should we ignore these attacks? If we do, they are likely to become stronger and stronger, as Church authorities who have ignored attacks on Catholic doctrine have found out.

No, we cannot ignore such things. However, it is crucial not to respond on the same level. When someone attacks us and appears to hate us, it is so easy to get dragged down into the mud with them. In other words, it is only human to hate and be angry in return. After all, the dissenters are attacking what we love most—the truths of our Catholic religion. If a man comes at you with a gun on the street or if he threatens your family, you can say theoretically that you love him but it is hard not to be outraged at your attacker as you seek to defend the values that you hold dear.

Nevertheless, in defending the Church's teaching, we must somehow develop the love of Christ Himself. It is Our Lord who tells us that we must love our enemies and do good even to those who persecute us. It is easy to love those who love us but we will only reflect Christ fully when we love those who are attacking us.

But love is not the same as capitulation. Love does not mean that we cease working for our Catholic beliefs. Nor does love mean that we fail to point out the tragic mistakes of those dissenters who are attacking Catholic doctrine and the equally tragic results of their dissent. Just as Christian love for the man coming at you with a gun does not mean that you let him shoot you, so love for Church dissenters does not mean that we cease doing everything in our power to stop them from turning others away from the teaching of Christ.

What has been said about our attitude toward Church dissenters can also be applied to Church authorities. It is only natural for us to look upon Church authorities as policemen who ought to be protecting us from attacks on Catholic teaching. Sometimes we will find to our joy that the Church authorities will do just that. At other times, however, some Church authorities may seem to allow the attack on Catholic doctrine to take place. Not only may they seem to stand by and do nothing, but sometimes they may even express anger at us and dismiss us impatiently if we ask them to check dissent. When this happens, it is very hard to avoid feeling disillusioned and bitter but somehow we must if the love of Christ is to show through us.

Such a Christian reaction to ridicule is one of the hardest lessons for us to learn—yet, if we are to succeed in defending Church doctrine, we must develop this attitude and demonstrate it again and again. As I write these words, I am thinking of one Catholic publication that is certainly very orthodox; it does much good work in promoting the true Catholic teaching. However, because the tone of many of its articles is often angry and even bitter, I have found that when I give this periodical to others, they usually remember only how angry the writers of the articles seemed to be. This is certainly unfair, because there is so much in this publication that is of value. The message? Sometimes our own strong feelings can keep us from reflecting Christ to others as we would want.

Have you not had similar experiences yourself? Suppose you come upon two people who are engaged in a heated argument. You know little of the actual situation. Do you not tend to react to their emotion rather than to the merits of what they are saying? In addition, is it not natural for you to want to avoid becoming involved in the controversy itself? You resist those who attempt to involve you because you shy away from the strong emotions that they are demonstrating.

In the same way, if our emotions appear too angry or vehement, we can actually block others from hearing what we are saying about Catholic doctrine. Our goal above all is to get others to experience what we ourselves have experienced—namely, the official teaching of the Church—to follow that teaching, to live it.

There is one way—and only one—in which we can succeed. People must see that this teaching has worked a change in us—that there is within us a goodness and a love. If they see that, then they will hear the words that we are trying to speak and they will be brought in increasing numbers to treasure the Church's official teaching.

PERSEVERANCE

We have written so far about love. A second quality is also most important—the quality of perseverance. Our Lord Himself (Luke 11:5-8) gives us the example of someone who, seeking help, knocks at the door of a friend in the middle of the night. The "friend" does not want to get up. "Do not bother me", he says. But the other person persists and—eventually—gets his way by becoming a nuisance. To quote Jesus directly:

> I tell you, if the man does not get up and give it to him for friendship's sake, persistence will be enough to make him get up and give his friend all he wants.

On another occasion in the Gospels (Luke 18: 1-5), Our Lord changes the example slightly and tells us about a judge who refuses to give a widow what is due to her in justice. But—just like the friend at the door—the widow makes a pest of herself. Our Lord quotes the judge as saying to himself:

> Since she keeps pestering me, I must give the widow her just rights, or she will persist in coming and worry me to death.

Our Lord Himself is telling us to "be a nuisance" if our cause is right! Notice that Jesus does not say that the person at the door and the widow were abusive or angry. But they persisted even to the point of being considered a pest, and this is the quality Christ Himself says we should have.

So, without becoming angry or bitter, we must keep on asking our bishops and our priests to promote the Church's official teaching. We must knock at the door again and again. Even if our bishops and priests consider us nuisances—even if we are rebuffed many times—we must continue to knock.

To act in this way, of course, involves personal sacrifice. In addition to our prayers to God, we must sacrifice if we are to achieve our goal. There are three kinds of sacrifices. First, there are the voluntary sacrifices—the little things we choose to give up as offerings to God. Second, there is the acceptance of any personal difficulties that we may encounter—for example, sickness. Third and perhaps most important, there is the willingness to accept ridicule, even ridicule that may come from within our parish by those people (perhaps even Church authorities) who will "put us down" for promoting the Papacy and the official teaching of the Church.

If we think about it, is not our sacrifice relatively small in comparison to Catholics of other times and places who have given up life itself because of their faithfulness to the Church's teaching? All God is asking us to do is to accept ridicule—to be laughed at by others. If we are so mocked, remember that nothing is happening to us that did not happen to Christ and the Apostles themselves. Our very willingness to put ourselves in such a situation can be the sacrifice Jesus wants and, if we respond to such ridicule with both Christian love and persistence, what we are saying will, through God's Grace, reach many Catholics and assist them as they struggle to be faithful to the official teaching of the Catholic Church.

Love and persistence. We will have to work on these two qualities for a lifetime. If we do, let us be confident that Christ's Grace can come to others through our activity.

2.
Strengthening Your Own Faith and the Faith of Your Family

In the Introduction to this book we set forth the threefold task that faces the Catholic who wishes to promote the Church's official teaching:

a. Strengthening and confirming his own faith
b. Passing on this faith to his children
c. Working within the parish and community at large

In this chapter we consider the specific steps we can take to strengthen our own faith and the faith of other members of our family. Previously we discussed the difference between doctrine and devotion. We must become knowledgeable about the Church's teaching (doctrine) and live these teachings in our lives (devotion). In strengthening our faith, therefore, we have to learn but then we have to respond with love. These two elements—doctrine and devotion—will be considered in this chapter.

A SPIRITUAL PROGRAM

One step that is very helpful in strengthening our own faith is to draw up a spiritual program for ourselves—a program of prayer and study that we will try to follow every day of our lives.

One such program has been recommended by Rev. Robert J. Fox in his pamphlet "Hope for the Isolated Catholic". This is an excellent pamphlet, published in 1983 by Christendom College Press, and it contains many valuable suggestions for Catholics trying to live the official teaching of the Church.

Fr. Fox suggests the following ten-point spiritual program:

1. *The Sign of the Cross*—beginning and ending our day by uniting ourselves with the Father, Son, and Holy Spirit.

2. *Morning prayers*—saying a prayer such as the Morning Offering to offer to Jesus through the Immaculate Heart of Mary all of our prayers, works, joys, and sufferings of the day. These morning prayers may be relatively short but they should never be omitted and they should remind us of the importance of dedicating our work of that day to the Lord.

3. *The Angelus*—the prayer that recalls the Incarnation of Our Lord and unites us with Our Blessed Lady.

4. *Aspirations*—short prayers such as "My Jesus Mercy" or "Immaculate Heart of Mary, pray for us now and at the hour of our death". These prayers can be said throughout the day whenever we have a moment. They can be said as we are waiting for a train or walking down the street. By such aspirations, we turn our minds to God for a moment or two and ask for His Help.

5. *The Sacred Liturgy of the Mass*—here Fr. Fox recommends Holy Communion each Sunday and frequent confession. The ideal, if at all possible, is to participate in the Mass daily and receive Jesus in Holy Communion. If one is not able to do this on a particular day, then it is most helpful to make what is known as a spiritual act of Communion—expressing the desire to receive Jesus on those days when we are not able to receive Him sacramentally. With respect to the sacrament of Penance, we are not obliged to confess our sins to a priest unless we have committed a serious sin. However, as part of a good spiritual program, it is recommended that we confess our sins at least once a month. Confession even of sins that are considered venial or past sins is an important way in which Christ comes to us. In fact, if we are able to do so, weekly confession would be desirable.

6. *The Daily Rosary*—preferably with the other members of your family. In praying the two beautiful prayers of the Our Father and the Hail Mary, we also meditate upon the important mysteries in the Life of Our Lord and Our Blessed Lady. We can say five decades of the Rosary at once or we and other members of our family can say them at different times of the day—perhaps at each meal time and the final two decades with night prayer.

7. *Visits to the Most Blessed Sacrament*—if it is possible, it is a wonderful practice to make a short visit daily to a Church and pray before the Blessed Sacrament. If this cannot be done daily, we should try to put aside at least one brief time during the week when we pray to our Divine Lord in the Most Blessed Sacrament.

8. *Spiritual reading*—Fr. Fox recommends at least 15 to 20 minutes per day. Here again we must discipline ourselves in order to do this

regularly. In spiritual reading, we will be studying both books of devotion and books of Catholic doctrine. The important thing is not how fast we get through each book but to read them as well as we can—to try to understand them—to pray over what we have read. In other words, we read and then we pause to meditate. We make our reading a form of prayer. As with all the other spiritual practices, we can do this not only by ourselves but as a family. We can choose spiritual readings that are helpful for all the members of our family and read them together at some time during the day.

9. *Evening prayer and examination of conscience*—before going to bed, we should say a few evening prayers of our choice. We should also briefly ask ourselves how we have done in the course of the day, thank God for the graces He has given to us, and pray for His Help for ourselves and our family in the future.

10. *Lay apostolate*—practical works for others. Our spiritual program should include working to help others in the promotion of Church teaching. We will discuss this later but we will usually find that in our parish and community there will be opportunities to do this. The first obligation for all parents is to pass on the faith to their own children. In addition many Catholics may be able to teach religious education classes or belong to the Legion of Mary or other such prayer groups.

The ten-point program recommended by Fr. Fox is an excellent one. Certainly we can, if we desire, add to it or change one item for another. For example, the prayer known as the Stations of the Cross can be a most helpful devotion in uniting ourselves with the Suffering of Jesus. As the Pope himself does, we should travel to shrines of Our Lady and join in special praying to Mary. It is also helpful for each of us to choose a few saints as special models—saints to whom we pray regularly for assistance. We should also pray to our guardian angel asking him to support us as we attempt to live the Christian life. Now the program presented here may seem to be a long one that takes up much time. However, this is an illusion. I would stress that it is possible to shorten or lengthen the program as our daily living requires. The important thing is that we pray regularly—that we attempt to deepen our love and our knowledge of what God has taught us through Christ.

If at times during our program of prayer and reading we feel distracted, we should never be discouraged. Sometimes people are disturbed that they go to Mass but often seem to be distracted—or they pray the Rosary but their minds wander. In such a situation we should not give up.

In God's eyes these "distracted" prayers can be very valuable. Even if we seem to "get nothing out of" such prayers in terms of our own emotional reaction, our effort to pray is what God wishes of us.

Having said that, it is certainly quite legitimate for us to choose prayers that inspire us in a special way. Because our own personalities are very different, some prayers will appeal to us that do not appeal to others. We might almost compare a spiritual program with a program of nutrition with respect to providing the body with food. A balanced diet must include the same elements—proteins, carbohydrates, starches, etc. However, within that particular framework, we can choose foods that we like over others that do not have the same appeal for us.

In the same way, we can choose prayers and spiritual readings that appeal to us—so long as our prayers and spiritual reading fulfill the basic purpose of a spiritual program—to deepen our knowledge of Christ and of His Teaching and to lead us closer to Him.

To consider further the example of food, some foods are very tasty. Others are not tasty but are important because they give us valuable nutrition. If one ate only the tasty foods, one might be in trouble. In the same way, certain spiritual readings will be very appealing to us. This may especially be the case with devotional works that arouse in us a strong and good emotional reaction. In contrast, some of the doctrinal works can appear to be dry because the emphasis here is on our intellect rather than on our emotional response. However, like the foods that are not tasty but are needed for valuable nutrition, these doctrinal works are also important. We should never judge the value of our spiritual reading on the emotional reaction alone—although it is certainly legitimate to try to find doctrinal works that also appeal to our emotions, just as we try to find nutritious foods that are also tasty.

In summary, our personal spiritual program should consist of a healthy balance between doctrinal works and devotional works—between books that appeal to our feelings and books that appeal to our intellect. Both types are necessary. As indicated previously, one of the problems with modern religious education programs—even those presented under Catholic auspices—is that they emphasize only religious feeling, and downplay the objective dogmatic reality (for example, the literal truth of doctrines such as Christ's Real Presence in the Eucharist). Without neglecting the importance of our emotional response, the spiritual program we set up for ourselves and our families must emphasize the Church doctrines themselves—especially since our children may not be receiving such an emphasis in the spiritual programs they are given elsewhere.

In our spiritual reading, it can be helpful to read more than one book at a time. For instance, we might spend fifteen minutes on Monday reading a good "devotional" book and fifteen minutes on Tuesday reading a good "doctrinal" book. In this way, we can alternate doctrinal and devotional books throughout the week.

Nor do we have to limit ourselves to books. There are many excellent cassette tapes available. We can play such a tape for ten or fifteen minutes a day, perhaps even in a family setting with the children present. As another family activity, each member of the family might read a different work and then share what they have learned with each other at a group meeting.

By such methods, we can both deepen our personal faith and share it with those closest to us. Reading doctrinal works—talking about them with other members of our family—these can be important ways to correct any lack of doctrinal emphasis that might exist in the parish religious education programs in which our children are enrolled. On the younger grade levels, it is usually not so much that such religious education programs are "anti-doctrinal" (in other words, that they explicitly deny important religious teachings of the Church) but that they are "non-doctrinal" (that they simply avoid all mention of important doctrinal truths). In this case, the doctrinal program that we develop in our homes will be the only way in which our children will learn important religious truths. With a good family program of devotion and doctrine, what we do in the home will be sufficient to overcome any defects that may exist in those school and parish programs in which our children are enrolled.

If a particular book or tape appeals to us but not to the other members of our family, we should accept this as natural. Just as the Church gives us many saints because She knows that each of us will have a special attraction to some saints but not to others, so we should expect a similar result with books of doctrine and devotion. Although all the works may be very good, some of us will be attracted to one author—to one set of books or tapes—while other members of our family will prefer something different. That is the reason it is so important to see what is available—to look around and to choose a variety of works in order to develop a good spiritual program for ourselves and for our entire family.

That, of course, leads us to the next question: Where do we find these good doctrinal and devotional works? Actually, they are all around us—although we may have to be careful in order to separate the good material from the works of Church dissenters who attack Church teaching.

For example, I recently went to a Catholic bookstore and found an excellent book that was orthodox, thorough, and interesting. Right next to this book on the very same shelf was another book by a prominent dissenter that ridiculed Church teaching. The first book is solid food for Catholics; the second is poison.

How do you know which is which? Actually, it is not that difficult. For example, in the pamphlet by Fr. Fox to which we previously referred ("Hope for the Isolated Catholic") he provides us with an extensive list of sources that we may use—including orthodox Catholic newspapers, magazines, newsletters, publishing houses, and distribution centers that feature doctrinally sound books and catechetical materials. This list is reprinted in an appendix to this book. Furthermore, as we read these materials, we will find that they in turn recommend other works. In time, we can build up a library of orthodox books and tapes.

The list that Fr. Fox devised was valid for 1983 when his pamphlet appeared. As the months and years go on, we will probably find that some of these works will go out of print. But others will come along. If we regularly read orthodox publications, we will be kept informed of these good new works.

BOOKS FROM THE PAST

In promoting the faith and understanding Church doctrine, it is important to consider not only current works but the great spiritual writings of the past.

In our modern age, we have a temptation to brand "out-of-date" anything that was not written within the last few years. Now there are certainly areas of knowledge (for example, advances in medicine and in other natural sciences) where books written 50 or 60 years ago would be almost totally out-of-date.

However, there are other areas of human activity in which age makes little difference. For instance, would anybody claim that the novels of Charles Dickens or the plays of William Shakespeare are out of date simply because they were written in previous centuries? To the contrary, such novels and plays may be far superior to anything written at the present time.

The reason that age matters little with such works is that they are not affected to any great extent by advances in factual knowledge that might have occurred since they were written. Instead, they are concerned with the fundamental problems and activities of men and women—things that do not change much throughout the centuries.

Because the great Catholic doctrinal and spiritual writings of the past can be as relevant to us today as the great works of literature, we have a rich heritage that we should not hesitate to draw upon.

In reading Catholic writers who may have lived 1000 or 1500 years ago, we may occasionally find a reference to something factual that is now outdated. Nevertheless, we should also find that at least ninety to ninety-five percent of such works remain as valuable and important for us today as they did for Catholics who lived at the time these books were written.

In the last chapter of this book I will be quoting St. Thomas à Becket and St. John Chrysostom. Their works inspire us today. Yet both saints lived hundreds of years ago—St. Thomas à Becket in the twelfth century, St. John Chrysostom in the fourth century more than 1500 years ago. What they say transcends time and is as valuable to us today as it was hundreds of years ago.

Once we learn to resist the modern prejudice that dismisses any work more than ten years old, we will discover literally thousands of books that will help us to live and understand our faith and to present it to others. At times we may have to search out such works in Catholic libraries, but the search will be well worth our time.

In summary, there is much orthodox Catholic writing available, but part of the work that we ourselves will have to do—part of the sacrifice we must make—is to search for those works that are both valuable in themselves and appealing to us. Then, if we are parents attempting to educate our children, we must look for similar works that will help our sons and daughters. (In this regard, it should be noted that Fr. Fox's pamphlet recommends regular catechetical programs that can be given to our children at various stages of their lives.)

One final word. As we try our best to live our faith and to pass it on to our children, we should avoid becoming overscrupulous or overanxious. We should always be confident that God will support us.

The effort involved may seem difficult. With God's Grace, it will not be. The prayer and work we put into drawing up a spiritual program for ourselves and the other members of our families will be an effort that will be blessed by Jesus Himself.

3.
How A Catholic Home Life Can Overcome Outside Pressures

Recall for a moment the quotations from Cardinal Wright and from Bishop Sheen which we presented at the beginning of our second book. Cardinal Wright compared some "Catholic" religious education programs to a fire that threatened to destroy the faith of the children sent to them. According to the Cardinal, parents often had to rescue their children from this fire. Bishop Sheen said that the atmosphere in "Catholic" colleges is sometimes so opposed to Church teaching that he tells parents to send their children to non-Catholic colleges (where they know they will have to fight for their faith) rather than to Catholic colleges (where the influence of Church dissenters can easily lead them to abandon their belief in Catholic doctrine).

If it is true that the very religious education programs devised to emphasize the importance of Catholic doctrine are now used to undermine belief in certain Catholic doctrines, how can parents protect the faith of their children? The programs in your parish may be controlled by Church dissenters. Or, if they are not, orthodox Catholic teachers and prominent dissenters may be found within the same school or religious education program. In this situation, your child is exposed to something like Russian roulette. On the one hand, he or she may, if your child is fortunate, find an excellent teacher who will be of great help in presenting Church teaching. On the other hand, if your child is not so lucky, your boy or girl may be placed in the hands of someone who will either show contempt for certain Church doctrines or who will totally ignore them.

The only way for parents to protect their children from this tragic situation is to develop the strongest possible Catholic atmosphere in the home—an atmosphere which promotes not only devotion but doctrine as well.

If they do so, parents can be confident that they have done everything in their power to promote the Catholic faith. It is true, of course, that every person is always free either to turn to Christ or to turn away from

Him. Even if parents have done their best, their children will always have the freedom to turn away. However, if the parents have prayed, if their religion has been a lived value in the home, if they have worked diligently to teach doctrine to their children, I think they will find in almost every instance that their children have developed the same love for Catholic teaching that the parents themselves have.

Here let me relate something from my own experience. In my pastoral work as a priest, I have had the opportunity to work with many couples who are active in the Right to Life movement. I have also had the opportunity to work with many Catholic couples who, while certainly supporting the Church's teaching on abortion, have not been active in the Right to Life movement.

I have noticed a very great difference in the way the children of these Catholic couples (namely, those personally active in the Right to Life and those not active) react to the abortion question.

In almost every case—and I am considering literally hundreds of examples—the children of parents active in the Right to Life movement share the strong convictions of their parents on abortion. They write term papers on the subject for their schools. At a certain stage, they ask to learn more about Right to Life. They speak up, they go to marches and they take part in other demonstrations on behalf of life.

Now it is interesting to me that these children invariably feel so strongly about abortion. There are two reasons it is of special note. First, the Right to Life parents are usually not thinking about their own sons or daughters participating in an abortion. Instead, the efforts of the parents are concentrated on convincing others outside of their family. But in their homes there is a very strong pro-life atmosphere and the children absorb it. The children hear their parents talking about this question. They see their parents making sacrifices to go to pro-life meetings. They realize that this is an area about which their parents feel deeply.

It is like being in a home where the parents love music or literature. The feeling is simply in the air. And, therefore, those parents who are seeking to advance the pro-life movement end up by having a tremendous blessing—namely, that their children share their own strong convictions on the subject.

A second reason I find this interesting is that, at first sight, one might expect the children to resent the involvement of their parents in the pro-life area. Often such involvement means that the parents are not able to spend as much time with their children as would otherwise be the case.

In addition, the children of active pro-life parents, like all children, go through a stage where they tend to react against their parents. Even in such conflict situations, however, it is noticeable that they do not react by reflecting the value that is lived so deeply by their mothers and fathers.

In contrast, those children from Catholic homes where opposition to abortion is not a "lived value" possess a very different attitude on the subject. In many cases, they will even support the pro-abortion position. By no means is this always true. However, if I were to use statistics, I would estimate that ninety-five percent of all Catholic children who come from a home where their parents are active in the pro-life movement share the strong conviction of their parents. In contrast, only about fifty percent of those children who come from a "good Catholic home"—but one in which the parents are not actively involved in Right to Life—share the view of their parents that abortion is wrong. Even if they do oppose abortion, these girls and boys rarely feel as strongly about the subject as those children who come from active Right to Life homes.

Why? The reason appears to be that in these other Catholic homes support of the Right to Life position is not a "lived value" in the way it is in those families where the parents are actively involved in the pro-life movement. I am sure that in many of these homes if one were to ask the parents "Do you support the Church's teaching on abortion?", the answer would be "Yes". However, the subject does not come up that often. As a result, the children are susceptible to pro-abortion influences from outside (from the media, from their schools, from their associates) in a way that the children of active pro-life families are not.

I might add that I noticed this difference only in connection with the abortion issue. On other matters of Church doctrine, the attitudes of children from strongly pro-life families did not seem much different from the attitudes of children from other good Catholic families. Thus, the children from the strong pro-life families would question Church doctrine on other subjects—but not on abortion.

Once again the reason appears to be that on subjects outside of abortion the parents active in the Right to Life movement were doing exactly what the other Catholic parents were doing. While they themselves believed in Catholic Doctrines, they did not feel confident to teach them and so they tended not to talk about these other doctrines but to leave it to the "experts" in the Catholic schools to teach Catholic doctrine to their children. They certainly wanted such teaching very much since many of the parents made sacrifices to send their children to Catholic schools. However, they themselves were not talking over the dinner table about the Real Presence of Our Lord in the Eucharist in the way that they were talking over the dinner table about abortion.

The lesson from all this? As with the abortion issue, if parents themselves become active in speaking out and teaching Catholic doctrine—if support of the Pope and the Church teaching becomes a lived value in their homes—they can have the same effect on their children with respect to all Catholic doctrine that the parents active in the Right to Life have with respect to abortion. If Catholic doctrine is a lived value in their homes, the atmosphere of grace and love will produce children who are so strongly loyal to the Pope and to Catholic teaching that even the insidious activity of dissenters in the Catholic school system will have little effect on them.

Please remember always that your children are taught not only by the formal lessons parents give them (although these are certainly necessary), but by what they see their mothers and fathers carrying out in practice. In the next chapter, we will consider how a group of Catholics can come together to work on the promotion of Catholic doctrine. What we will say there is similar to what people in the pro-life movement have done to promote opposition to abortion. If parents are so active—if they become deeply involved in the struggle to promote the teaching of the Church— they will face many discouragements and will be called on to make many sacrifices. But they will have one great reward. Their children will see what they are doing—their children will observe that their support of the Pope and of Catholic teaching is a lived value of great importance—and, in almost every case, the parents will succeed in communicating this value to their children.

We have been discussing the promotion of Catholic doctrine. What we have said applies also to Catholic devotion. Here many parents do feel competent and they already have a number of home religious practices in which the other members of the family take part.

As outlined previously, parents should encourage their children to join with them in prayer, in visiting shrines of Our Lady, in attending daily Mass, and even in reading together a Catholic book of spiritual value. Naturally, as the children grow older, the readings and even some of the devotions may change. Furthermore, people in the same family will have a different preference when it comes to devotions. However, this should certainly not keep the family from praying together and from joining together in religious projects undertaken as a group.

At a certain point in time (and, if the promotion of Catholic doctrine is a lived value in your family, the children will probably be aware of this much earlier than you might expect) your sons and daughters will have to be informed that even in Catholic institutions there are those who will not share their strong convictions in support of the Pope and Church teaching. Unless they are so informed, they can be caught unaware when they attend these schools and find teachers questioning the Catholic faith.

It is certainly advisable, of course, for parents to try to find both Catholic religious education programs and Catholic schools where the influence of the dissenters does not exist. As you become active in the promotion of Catholic doctrine, you will become aware of such institutions. (In Fr. Fox's pamphlet, for example, he lists colleges and religious education programs that are completely orthodox and that promote Church teaching most effectively.)

However, it may not always be possible to avoid the influence of dissenters. They may be active in your parish or writing for your diocesan newspaper. Despite this unfortunate fact, if your home environment is strong enough, your children's faith will be protected.

In a sense it is easier when your children are in the lower grades, because they usually face not so much an active assault on Church doctrine but simply the omission of doctrine that the dissenters feel is not meaningful. In the higher grades, however, the dissenters often openly attack Church teaching.

For instance, one of the tragedies I have witnessed concerns a pre-Cana program in a diocese. This diocese has what appears on the surface to be a very good rule that couples who are about to be married must attend a pre-Cana program to learn about the teachings of the Church relative to marriage. The only trouble with this rule is that the dissenters control the program. In the actual situation, therefore, Catholic men and women are being forced to attend pre-Cana programs in which the teaching of the Pope on matters such as contraception is called into question.

What a perversion! Catholic couples are told that if they seek to avoid these programs then the Church will not marry them because they are "not properly educated". However, if they attend, then they are forced to listen to a barrage of information designed to lead them to reject the Church's teaching and to accept the view of the dissenters instead.

Faced with such a situation, Catholics should write letters to the bishop—and, if necessary—to the Pope himself. It is a grave injustice to force Catholics to attend these programs.

Despite such activity by the dissenters, if parents have emphasized the support of the Pope in their homes, their children can survive these attacks upon their faith. The general rule is to avoid such attacks whenever possible. If a situation develops where they cannot be avoided, prayer and sacrifice and preparation—as in all cases where those living the true Catholic faith are persecuted (and forcing Catholic couples to listen to attacks upon the official Church teaching is a kind of persecution)—can protect Catholics from the assault being made upon their precious gift of the Catholic faith.

In conclusion, what we have been describing is a situation in which the outside environment (in this case, sadly, even a Catholic parish or school) is at least to some degree hostile to certain Catholic doctrines. In such a situation, Catholics can respond to the challenge in one of two ways. They can give in to the hostile environment. On the other hand, they can dig in with more determination than ever—work even more strongly than before to overcome the outside difficulties—and that is the course of action I recommend to Catholic parents with respect to their children. Pray for them unceasingly. Offer sacrifices for them. Love them. Teach them. Most of all, in the community of your family set up an environment in which there is a lived value of promoting *both* Catholic doctrine and Catholic devotion. Do everything in your power—and then trust in God.

4.
Working Within the Church Community At Large

As we turn our thoughts to the ways we can promote the teaching of the Church even outside of our own family, let us first distinguish what we are about from what we are not about. "What we are about" is above all to promote the official teaching of the Church. In support of that teaching, we would also like to encourage the many Catholics who are doing good—from the Pope himself to the Catholic next door who wants to live his faith. In addition to encouraging orthodox Catholics, we may have to face the problem of dissent. What is the best way to defend the Pope when we encounter dissenters who are attempting to discredit his teaching? In other words, we may have to fight the bad in addition to promoting the good. This means defending Catholics from the attacks that the dissenters will make upon the teaching of the Church and to some extent exposing the mistakes of the dissenters.

This is "what we are about". Now let us consider "what we are not about" when we speak of promoting the Church's teaching.

Here it might be good to review quickly what has been covered in our previous books. Our goal is to promote the Church's teaching as the Church Herself teaches it. We are especially concerned with promoting that teaching of the Pope which is binding with respect to matters of faith and morals. As we discussed in Book I, this can involve not only the teachings of the "extraordinary magisterium: but also teachings of the "ordinary magisterium".

In promoting the authority of the Pope, we are not concentrating so much on the Holy Father as an individual. Certainly we hope that the Pope is holy and has all the characteristics of a strong leader. Such characteristics can be invaluable.

Nevertheless, even if the Pope did not have these personal characteristics, he would still be the Pope. What we are defending above all is the office of the Papacy in the Church. In our first book we used the example of a judge or a policeman to point out that the authority possessed by these officers does not depend upon their personality or talents. Even if we do not like these individuals personally, we are obliged to obey when they are properly exercising the authority of their offices.

In summary, in promoting the office of the Papacy, we will often in fact be promoting the Pope as a kind of Catholic "hero". We do this because we will usually find the Pope to be an inspiring person and it is only natural for people to be brought to a belief through the personal qualities of those who advocate it. That is probably the way we ourselves learned about our religion and it is also the way we teach others, and it is the reason that we too must always try to be as holy and generous and Christ-like as we can.

At the same time we must keep in mind that God has not necessarily guaranteed that all those who occupy positions of authority in the Church will always be holy men. Referring to this question, St. Augustine wrote over 1500 years ago that if a time arises when the shepherds in the Church are not good people, we should follow what they say while rejecting what they personally do. In other words the Divine guarantee is to protect the Church's teaching. If, as seems to have happened at times during the Middle Ages, a particular Pope is worldly, God will protect the Church so that this Pope will not falsify Catholic doctrine. (I might add that in addition to the supernatural, there is even a certain natural logic in this since a pope or bishop concerned primarily with worldly matters is most unlikely to be making statements on the Real Presence of Christ in the Eucharist or other doctrinal subjects.)

Finally, in addition to supporting the authority of the Pope, orthodox Catholics also support the authority of the bishops. However, it is important to remember that, as Vatican II taught explicitly, the bishops must be united with the Pope in their teaching. An individual bishop or a group of bishops has no power whatever to oppose or modify the doctrinal teaching of the Pope.

In defending the teaching of the Pope, we are talking about his religious teaching on faith and morals. We are not talking about the views of the Pope on sports or politics or any subject outside the scope of his office.

And, of course, what we just said about the teaching of the Pope can also be applied to ourselves. In seeking to promote the teaching of the Church, we must be careful to promote just that—not our own personal views on subjects of faith and morals.

For example, I know of one organization that staunchly upholds the doctrinal teaching of the Holy Father but also promotes certain political views as well. While any organization has a right to do this if it wishes, a problem is obviously created when the same group seeks to promote both politics and doctrine. The Church's doctrinal teachings are binding. All Catholics have an obligation to follow them. To the contrary, political views are optional so long as we are referring to a political view that does not in itself go contrary to a matter of faith or morals.

When an organization stands not only for Church teaching but also for a political viewpoint, it becomes difficult for Catholics with different political views to work with this organization even if they share with them the desire to support the doctrinal teaching of the Church. We will discuss this later under "Organization" when we consider the importance of setting up groups in which all Catholics who agree on the importance of official Church doctrine can work together—regardless of their differences on other matters.

WHAT WE COULD - AND EVEN OUGHT TO - BE ABOUT
(but always secondary to the essentials of Church teaching)

In supporting the Pope, we have been considering "what we are about" and "what we are not about". However there is a third area. It can be described as "what we *can* be about—although always secondary to the essentials of Church teaching themselves".

We might begin our discussion of this area by recalling that it is not only in politics where there is liberty among Catholics. Even on many religious matters, the Church Herself allows options. The Church Herself recognizes that there can be differences of opinion.

In our first book we made a distinction between what could change within the Church and what could not. Among the things that can change are Church customs and Church laws. Even though they can change, they may still be very important. If so, it is also important for Catholics to express their views on such matters. In fact, many times it is a change in a Church custom or law that will disturb Catholics most because it involves a change in what they see and experience on the parish level.

Behind the question of whether a Church law should or should not be changed, there usually is an important prudential judgment about the best course of action to take at the current moment. The fundamental question always is: In presenting the Church's unchanging doctrinal teaching, what particular "disciplinary" policy is most helpful in our time and age?

While there is an obligation for all Catholics to follow the current Church discipline, Catholics do have the freedom to try to convince authorities to change Church laws. It is even legitimate for us to speak out publicly on such matters except in those instances where the Pope—for the good of the Church—may have asked that public discussion cease.

Therefore, because the Church's discipline is so important, groups of Catholics should be active in expressing their views on proposed changes. Let me take some specific examples.

Suppose that the bishops of our country are discussing whether or not to reduce the number of holy days (or, to put it more precisely, to remove the obligation of attending Mass on these days). Such a question actually came before the bishops recently. I myself urged Catholics to write to the bishops in support of retaining all the present holy days. Nevertheless, it is certainly true that those who might have favored the opposite approach—those who wished to see the number of holy days reduced—were in no way disloyal. They were exercising a legitimate freedom—namely, the freedom to urge Church authorities to change a Church law.

Such Catholics are obviously very different from those who question the Real Presence of Christ in the Eucharist. People who challenge Church doctrines such as the Real Presence are abusing freedom because all Catholics have an obligation in conscience to believe in these unchanging Church teachings. In contrast, the discussion about the number of Holy days involves a question as to the best policy to pursue at the present moment in order to emphasize the importance of the Mass. While I personally thought it would have been a serious mistake to reduce the number of Holy days—and while I urged Catholics to speak up for the present discipline—I also recognize that those Catholics who advocated a change in this matter were within their rights in doing so.

As we become involved in Church discussions, it is always important to keep in mind the great difference between those Catholics who advocate a change in discipline and those who advocate a change in doctrine. Sometimes, in their desire to support the Church, loyal Catholics can easily forget about this distinction and treat those who advocate a change in Church laws as if they were in the category of those who dissent on matters of faith.

Because there is so much dissent around us—dissent on vital matters of Church doctrine—we may constantly have to resist the temptation to assume that almost everyone is against us—to see unlawful dissent even in situations where we are actually faced with a legitimate expression of opinion. In Fr. Fox's pamphlet, he refers to this matter by observing that he himself, while certainly an orthodox priest, has had the experience of being criticized by Catholics who were stricter than Rome itself.

Fr. Fox gives the example of a layman who criticized him for wearing a black suit and Roman collar and who insisted that he was obliged to wear a thirty-three button cassock. To quote Fr. Fox directly: "Now, if he could present to me an authentic Papal document that I was to wear a cassock with thirty-three buttons at all times (even to bed), I would do so immediately! Indeed I, as a conservative priest, receive sufficient advice from ultraconservatives who misrepresent the Church, that if I were to attempt to enforce their unofficial directives I would soon lose my sanity."

None of this is meant to deny that the Church's greatest need in the present crisis is for Catholics who will speak up for orthodoxy. Indeed, to help such Catholics is the whole purpose of these books. What we are saying here, however, is that we must never attempt to be "more Catholic than the Pope". We must recognize that there are areas of legitimate freedom. With respect to a matter of Church discipline, all Catholics are obliged to follow the current discipline but they do have the right to advocate change. With respect to defying Catholic doctrine, nobody has the right to advocate change.

Having made this distinction, we now find ourselves facing what seems at first glance to be a dilemma. Let us illustrate this apparent dilemma by taking a crucial question of Church discipline—namely, the celibacy of the clergy. Even those who most strongly defend clerical celibacy realize that it falls in the category of Church law. In other words it could be changed. In fact, even at the present time, the Church occasionally allows a rare exception to the general rule of clerical celibacy. For example, when a married Protestant minister converts to the Catholic Church and asks to become a Catholic priest, the Church will often grant his request and ordain him even though he is married. In other words, the rule of clerical celibacy is dispensed for him.

While the Church's law of clerical celibacy could be changed tomorrow—and the Pope could permit all priests to be married—this does not mean it should be changed. To the contrary, the Holy Father is convinced that there is great spiritual value in the law of clerical celibacy. For that reason, the Pope believes that the present discipline should definitely be retained.

Nevertheless, a loyal Catholic could favor permitting Catholic priests to marry. The advocacy could even be public so long as it were done with respect for the Pope and so long as the Holy Father had not requested that such public discussion cease.

It is at this point that those of us working for Catholic doctrine face our apparent dilemma. On the one hand, a disciplinary matter such as priestly celibacy is most important. Naturally, we want to speak out on such a question. Many of us will wish to defend the present law especially when we see other Catholics suggesting a change. In such a situation, how can we remain silent?

But, if we do speak out, how can we work together with those Catholics who may be in complete agreement with us on faith and morals but who would like to see a change in the Church's discipline on priestly celibacy? It is most important that all orthodox Catholics who believe in the Church's doctrinal teaching be able to join together.

Can this be done if our organization is also taking a strong stand on a disciplinary matter on which orthodox Catholics may disagree? In such a case it seems inevitable that there will be tension and infighting within the group as people with different views on the disciplinary matter work for their position.

When the question is put this way, it would appear that the solution would be for our group to avoid taking a stand on all disciplinary questions and to emphasize only doctrine. But, as we have just said, disciplinary matters can be very important. Furthermore, other members of our group will almost certainly speak out on disciplinary questions especially if they think a basic value is involved.

Thus, our apparent dilemma: If you want to work with all those who agree with you on doctrine, you will have to avoid speaking out on matters of discipline (holydays, clerical celibacy, etc.). But, if you do avoid speaking out, you will not be contributing to some of the most important decisions faced by the Church.

I call this an "apparent dilemma" because there is an answer. The "dilemma" assumes that orthodox Catholics can work with each other only if they come together in one group. This is certainly one possible organizational model. However, as we will discuss later when considering how to organize groups to support Church teaching, it is probably better for orthodox Catholics to develop a number of smaller groups instead of one large group. Each group would have its own identity and its own right to make decisions on those matters where the Church permits a diversity of views. Nevertheless, they would frequently communicate with each other by a process that is sometimes referred to as "networking". Thus, the small groups could join together in common projects on matters involving essential areas such as Church doctrine.

On subjects where the Church allows liberty—such as advocating or opposing a change in Church discipline—some of the smaller groups might choose to become very active. Others might decide to avoid these areas entirely. Those groups that did choose to be active—for instance, in support of the present discipline on priestly celibacy—would communicate with other small groups who felt the same way. However, if an orthodox Catholic disagreed with these groups on such a disciplinary matter, he or she could join one of the other small groups that confined itself to doctrinal questions (or even form a new group since each small group would have perhaps five or ten people in it). In this way, one could continue to work with all other orthodox groups on essential doctrinal matters while retaining the freedom to act differently in areas where the Church permits liberty.

HELPING THE CHURCH TO MAKE DECISIONS ON NON-DOCTRINAL SUBJECTS

Promoting Church doctrine should always be our prime concern. This task should occupy most of the time and resources we can give to Church matters. Nevertheless, orthodox Catholics should make full use of the freedom the Church allows them to express their views on non-doctrinal questions. The basic reason our involvement is so important is that when we are considering what is the best policy for the Church to adopt at a particular moment in Her history, there are usually both arguments for the proposed policy and arguments against it. In such situations, the entire Church can benefit from an intelligent discussion as to whether the advantages of the policy outweigh the disadvantages.

In Book II we saw this with respect to St. Paul and St. Peter. St. Peter's decision not to eat with the Gentiles was a practical policy that had a good effect and a bad effect. He was conscious of the good effect because people favoring the policy had communicated with him. He was not nearly so sensitive to the bad effect—at least until Paul spoke out.

The same can be true today with respect to any major policy decisions made by the Pope and the bishops.

Suppose, for example, that the Holy Father is invited to speak in a Protestant church. Should he accept the invitation? In making his decision, the Pope must weigh a possible good effect against a possible bad effect.

The good effect is that accepting such an invitation might help to create a situation in which past divisions within the Christian community could be overcome. It could be a dramatic way to express love for the Protestant community.

However, one can also see a possible bad effect. Acceptance of such an invitation might create the false impression that one church is as good as another.

Therefore, in judging whether to accept such an invitation or to decline it, the Holy Father has to consider whether the good effect or the bad effect is most likely to occur. What he is trying to judge is how this action will be perceived by the community in general. If it will be perceived as an act of friendship and not as implying that one church is as good as another, then he certainly should go. On the other hand, if it will create a false impression, then he should decline. To make this decision it is important for the Pope to be able to judge the public impact of the action he is contemplating. He can only do this if we make our views known.

The same can be said about virtually any other proposed change in a Church custom or Church law. Why do some Catholics advocate a change in the present discipline of clerical celibacy? A frequently given reason is that they believe such a change would increase greatly the number of priests. This is a good effect.

However, there is also a likely effect that is not good. Throughout Church history—in fact, stated in the Scriptures itself—there has been a strong emphasis on the religious value of consecrated celibacy. Priests give up marriage not because the married state is bad or imperfect (for matrimony is one of the seven sacraments of Christ) but as a way of emphasizing that there is a loving relationship with God that reaches out to all and transcends the present. Recognizing the great value of consecrated celibacy, the sacrifice that is made to Christ Himself of something most good, the Church asks Herself: If priests were permitted to marry, would this real value of consecrated religious celibacy tend to disappear from the Church?

In other words, we must compare a good effect with a bad effect.

What is true of proposed Church policies is also true of every one of our own actions. In deciding what we should do, we will constantly be weighing a good effect against a bad effect. Suppose we are in a parish where dissent to the teachings of the Holy Father is promoted by some Catholics—even by certain sisters or priests. Should we point this out to other Catholics within the parish or will this only make things worse? What are the good and bad effects of public criticism? What are the good and bad effects of remaining silent?

We can even ask the same question—although in a different way— with respect to our reaction to policy decisions made by the Pope and the bishops. To use the example just given, suppose that the Pope decides it is best to speak in the Protestant church. We ourselves sincerely believe he has made a mistake. In other words, we believe that the bad effect will outweigh the good. But what should we do now? Should we publicly urge the Pope to change his decision once he has made it? If so, to what extent?

On the one hand, we certainly have the right to express a view that is contrary to the adopted policy—providing again that we do so in a respectful manner and that it is not an area where the Pope has asked that public discussion cease. After all, this is what the Apostle Paul himself did. Voicing such a different opinion can even be encouraging to Catholics who may be disturbed by what is happening. It can be beneficial for them to know that this is a matter on which they are allowed to disagree. Furthermore, if we do not speak out, will we be able to have an impact with respect to any such future decisions?

That is the possible good effect of speaking out. As to the bad effect, will we play into the hands of doctrinal dissenters if we appear to disagree with the Pope? Will many Catholics receive the impression, despite our intentions and even despite our attempts to explain, that our own actions show that "dissent" is acceptable? Will the average Catholic grasp the distinction between dissenting on binding Church teaching on faith and morals (which is not allowed) and disagreeing with a policy in the practical order (where it is permissible for loyal Catholics to disagree)? If not, would it be better to keep quiet?

In other words, the problem we face is similar to the problem faced by the Pope—judging the reaction of the public. The Pope had to decide whether his acceptance of an invitation to preach in a Protestant church would give people the impression (despite his intentions and despite any clarifying statements) that one church is as good as another. We have to

decide whether our public disagreement with a Church policy would give
people the impression (despite our intention and despite any clarifying
statements) that dissent to the Holy Father's doctrinal decisions is acceptable.

In such situations there is no clear-cut answer as to whether the good
effect will outweigh the bad effect. Usually these matters have to be
decided case by case. In some circumstances it may definitely be better
for Catholics to keep quiet with respect to a policy decision made by
Church authorities—even though it involves an area where they are free
to disagree. At other times, it may be important to speak out—although
always with respect.

What we have said here should re-emphasize the necessity of educat-
ing all Catholics as to the key distinction between doctrinal dissent and
policy dissent. This is especially the case because doctrinal dissenters
often try to confuse Catholics by hiding behind policy dissenters. In
addition, it should be pointed out that even if we disagree with a Church
policy because we fear the bad effect will outweigh the good effect, it is
important for us to explain to others what the Pope actually intended. For
example, suppose we personally think it would have been better for the
Pope not to have accepted the invitation to preach in the Protestant
church. Even if this is our opinion, there is still a job for us to do—
namely, to explain to people what the Pope actually intends and to
remove any false impression that the Pope's action means that one
religion is as good as another.

In other words, we may be working for a change in a Church policy
because we sincerely believe its bad effects outweigh its good effects.
However, so long as it is the official Church policy, loyalty to the Pope
should lead us to do whatever we can to make the policy succeed. That
means doing everything in our power to increase the policy's good effects
while minimizing its bad effects.

For the last few pages we have been emphasizing the importance of
distinguishing between areas that involve Church doctrine and areas that
involve Church discipline. Some issues clearly involve doctrine. Other
issues clearly involve discipline.

Yet there is also a third category. There are some areas where a
dispute may arise as to whether a question involves only Church discipline or an unchanging Church doctrine as well. In these areas, one must
be very careful in advocating a change in the Church's discipline because
it is by no means clear that the decision of the Church is not a doctrinal

one. An example of this area would be the discussion about women priests. The question of the ordination of women is very different from the question of optional celibacy for priests. With respect to priestly celibacy, all concede that the Church could allow married priests if She wished. With respect to the ordination of women, the basic question is whether Christ left this matter to the discretion of the Church or whether the fact that He ordained only men means that the Church has no power to act differently.

On such a question, it is important for loyal Catholics to remove the false impression that critics of the Church's position constantly strive to give. The priesthood is an office within the Church. As we discussed earlier, we must always distinguish an office from the holiness of the person who occupies the office. Priests are not necessarily holier than lay people. Or, to put it with reference to the current discussion, women are not necessarily less holy than men simply because women are not priests. Holiness, the most important consideration of all, involves our personal relationship with God through Christ. If women are not ordained as priests, this says nothing about their holiness or their talents or their intelligence.

We can see this immediately when we consider that the holiest, most talented, and most intelligent follower of Christ who ever existed was Our Blessed Mother. Yet she was not a priest.

There have been other women in Church history who have, as far as we can judge, been far holier, more talented, and more intelligent than almost any priest we could think of. Women such as St. Teresa of Avila or St. Catherine of Siena come to mind. None of these women ever sought to become priests. They believed only men could be ordained. Yet they never regarded this as an insult to women.

But some might say: "Well, it is true that Christ ordained only men, but that was a cultural accident. At the time Our Lord lived, it would not have been socially acceptable for Him to ordain women. In our age, however, it can be done."

Apart from the fact that Our Lord did many things that were not considered socially acceptable at the time (and, therefore, social acceptability would hardly seem to be a reason that He would not ordain women), it should be pointed out that this is the very question the Church must decide. Is it only a custom that men alone are ordained or is it something essential and established by Christ Himself? It is the responsibility of the Pope, exercising his teaching office under the guidance of the Holy Spirit, to decide such questions.

At the very least, the Church's teaching throughout its history creates a strong presumption that the question of the ordination of women involves not only Church discipline but also Church doctrine. Repeatedly the Popes have taught that the reason women are not ordained is that the Church believes this is an area where Christ did not grant the Church the power to make any changes. Therefore, the decision of the Pope is not a disciplinary decision but a doctrinal decision, and the Pope should not be attacked—as he often is today—by a clever public relations campaign that falsely attempts to brand him as anti-woman.

Could the Church's teaching change? On this question, some Catholics believe that the Church has already made a final and binding doctrinal decision. If so, no change is possible. Other Catholics (and here I am not talking about doctrinal dissenters but about loyal Catholics) believe that a final and binding decision on the doctrinal aspects of the women's ordination question has not yet been made although they concede that Church teaching is definitely leaning strongly in a certain direction. (In our first book, we pointed out that there is a category of Church teaching in which the Popes indicate strongly what a certain position is likely to be but do not yet make a final and binding doctrinal decision.)

Whether a final and binding Church doctrine already exists or whether the teaching is simply leaning strongly towards such a final and binding decision, the current situation on the ordination of women is clear. Women are not ordained because the Church believes this is an area where She has no power to make any changes—not because the Church believes women are less capable than men.

In this situation, it is important for those who are loyal to the Church's teaching to present the true reasons for it. Unfortunately many Catholics—including, sadly, some bishops—give lip-service to the teaching but make no effort whatsoever to explain it. Sisters, priests, and even some bishops can frequently be heard to say that "maybe some day" the Church will change Her position and that they see "no doctrinal problems" in ordaining women. (Rarely, if ever, will they mention that the Church Herself does see "doctrinal problems".) Thus, they create the impression that the Pope's position is based on a rather silly and archaic custom. Such priests, sisters, and bishops save their own popularity but at the price of making the Church look foolish. Because it would involve a certain personal inconvenience to them, they duck the question instead of presenting the reasons for the Church's position.

Of the millions of Catholics, only a very small percentage will ever become priests. Even fewer will become bishops. So what? The great news of our Christian religion is that God is among us and present to all of us. Whether we are priest or layman—no matter what office we exercise in the Church—Jesus has given Himself to us. The truly important and wondrous reality is that each of us has been called by God to union with Him through Christ. As for the question of women's ordination, the example of Our Blessed Lady, of Teresa of Avila, and of other great women saints should make it clear that personal holiness—not ordination—is the goal toward which all Catholics should strive.

5.
Forming An Effective Group To Promote Church Teaching

As mentioned previously, Catholics who agree on the important goal of defending Church teaching can disagree on strategy. Whenever this happens, it is very easy for such Catholics to fight each other. They can even spend all or most of their time on internal conflicts rather than on what they wanted to do in the first place—namely, to act effectively in support of the Church's teaching.

How can a group avoid getting bogged down in such internal conflicts?

In the last chapter we made a suggestion that we will now develop a little further. Small but effective organizations should be set up to work for Church teaching. This, of course, leads us to a question that is in itself a matter of strategy. Is it better to have one large organization to work for Church doctrine or a number of small ones? If there are one hundred people in our area who are willing to work for the Pope and Catholic doctrine, should the hundred people all be in one group? Or should we set up ten more-or-less separate groups of ten people apiece?

Like all questions of strategy, this is a question about which loyal Catholics can sincerely disagree. There are advantages in a big organization. There are advantages in a small organization. A large organization can have a great amount of influence and can appear to be very impressive. On the other side, it is often true that the bigger an organization becomes the slower it responds to any problem that arises. Big organizations have a tendency to get bogged down in "red tape". As a result, a large organization may be very hard to move.

In contrast, a small organization often lacks the power or prestige of a big organization. Because it can move rapidly, however, it can usually cover more ground in a shorter time. To use an illustration, it is somewhat like building one large battleship or a hundred canoes. Depending upon what we desire to accomplish, there is a value in each approach.

More important than the matter of size is the key question for any organization: How can we make it effective? I have had an experience that I imagine many others have shared. On the one hand, I have participated in a number of fine organizations that accomplished much. On the other hand, I have also belonged to groups that never seemed to accomplish anything. In some of these ineffective organizations a sharp conflict developed between the members of the group. In other ineffective organizations, there was little fighting but the group seemed to talk and talk and never act. Even if the people in such groups were intelligent and capable, nothing ever seemed to come from their meetings.

Why are some organizations effective while others are not?

In considering this question, let me begin by giving two examples from my own experience—one of a parish organization that was effective; the other of a parish organization that was not.

Probably the best organization that I ever joined was a Vincent de Paul group that met weekly in a certain parish. The group consisted of only five people. When they came together each week, the meetings were quite informal. The discussion usually began with a number of friendly comments—even with the telling of a few jokes. After a few moments, however, the group would consult a list of the poor families within the parish to be contacted. In the course of the meeting, a decision would be made as to which member would visit each of the poor families that needed help. The next week each member would give an informal report on the work he had accomplished.

Over the course of a year, this Vincent de Paul group visited literally hundreds of families. Within their parish, these five individuals did a great amount of invaluable work for the poor. At the same time, they enjoyed their weekly meetings with each other.

In contrast, that same parish had a parish council which did not work nearly so well. On the parish council there were twenty-five people. The meetings were much more formal than those held by the Vincent de Paul organization. In addition, they lasted much longer since there was far more talking. Ironically, however, the parish council accomplished much less work.

In considering the differences between these two groups—as I try to understand why one was effective and the other was not—I notice first that the Vincent de Paul group was action-oriented. In addition, the meeting itself was not the place where the work was done. Rather the work was accomplished by each member between the meetings. The purpose of the meeting itself was two-fold. First, it encouraged the members of the Vincent de Paul group by giving them a chance to report on what they had accomplished as well as an opportunity to socialize with others who were doing similar work. Second, the weekly Vincent de Paul meeting enabled the group to divide up the future work that each member would undertake.

Thus, every member of the Vincent de Paul group went away from every meeting with a specific task to be done, something that they knew was within their ability to perform.

In addition, the Vincent de Paul group was small enough (only five members) so that everyone in the group could take an active part in speaking at the meetings. The informality was such that it was un-important who held the title of chairman since all the members were on a more-or-less equal level. As a result, there was no struggle within the group for honors or for titles or for power. Instead, all the effort was directed outward toward the problem of helping the poor people in the parish.

In contrast, the parish council group differed on almost all of these points. First, the meeting itself was usually the place where the parish council thought it could do important work. Members of the parish council usually did not go away with a specific assignment to be accom-plished for the next meeting. Second, the parish council tended to be "talk oriented" rather than "action oriented". By that I mean that most of the parish council's time was taken up in passing resolutions which were often carefully worded and subject to a process of amendment. Or, if the wording of resolutions was not being debated, hours were spent in discussing parish problems, but without the concrete action steps directed toward the outside that existed in the Vincent de Paul group. Therefore, while those parishioners who did not attend the Vincent de Paul meeting would frequently observe the members of that group working with the poor, few, if any, parishioners would notice any particular results emerg-ing from the parish council because the members of that group did not usually work on specific tasks between the meetings.

In addition, the parish council meeting was so large that many people did not play an active role. In practice, four or five people did most of the talking while the other twenty people were relatively silent.

Another difference between the parish council and the Vincent de Paul organization was that the latter group was confident it could solve its problems. Each member of the Vincent de Paul group was convinced that he had the expertise and the ability to do what was needed with respect to the task assigned him. In contrast, an atmosphere of frustration often existed at the parish council meetings. Many members felt that some of the problems were beyond their ability to solve. They were not sure of anything specific that they could do in these areas.

Finally, the title of chairman was a prestigious one within the parish council. As a result, there was a spirited election process both with respect to the chairmanship of the council itself and with respect to the chairmanship of various committees. In time, blocs began to emerge as some members joined together to work against others. This led to sharp internal conflict within the council itself. The battles would usually continue from one meeting to the next as both sides struggled for "control" of where the council was going. As opposed to the Vincent de Paul group, titles and honors and internal power were very important. With the council engrossed either in a spirited contest over internal power or in lengthy debate over resolutions, little effective action resulted.

Using the example of these two groups, I would suggest that the following qualities can be of great help in forming an effective organization:

1. It should be "action oriented" rather than "discussion oriented".

2. It should be clear to all the members that the basic work has to be done outside the meeting. The purpose of the meeting is not to do the work itself but to report about the progress that has been made, to socialize among the members of the group, and to divide up the work that should be done in the future.

3. The work involved should be a specific task that each member feels competent to perform.

4. The group should be small enough so that all the members can participate actively.

5. The efforts of the group should be focussed on outside work—rather than on internal discussions in which the members of the group talk to themselves.

6. Internal conflict should be avoided as far as possible by minimizing the importance of prestige, titles, and power within the group.

7. As in the Vincent de Paul group, members should freely agree on the tasks which they wish to undertake (rather than having a situation in which some members attempt to tell others what they must do.)

It is to fulfill these qualities that I recommend small groups. They can do smaller projects themselves and, by communicating with each other by newsletters and other means, they can also join together in undertaking the larger projects.

In a large group most people inevitably tend to sit back. They think that the "officers" are taking care of the problems and their task is only to respond when called upon.

As a group grows bigger, more and more power will be centered in a relatively few officers. This in turn means that members will be increasingly tempted to fight each other on matters of strategy. For instance, if a large group has raised thousands of dollars, a conflict is almost inevitable over how the money should be used. In addition, a large group tends to stabilize at a set number while small groups can keep on multiplying. The large group also has the problem of trying to get everyone together at the same time for its meetings. When people begin to miss meetings, their active participation in the group sags and they usually start to drop out.

The small group concept solves the problem we discussed earlier— differences of strategy. We talked about this in connection with the question of whether a group should stay only with questions of doctrine or take a stand also on important matters of Church discipline. A small group allows the freedom to go either way while avoiding conflict with those who might feel differently.

A similar problem of strategy arises with respect to this question: In working for Church doctrine, should we concentrate exclusively on promoting the good? Or should we also speak out against abuses where they exist?

Here again we can present arguments for both sides. If we do not speak out against abuses, they can catch people unawares. On the other hand, if we do speak out, there may be many Catholics who will feel they cannot join our group. For example, suppose that the diocesan newspaper regularly propagates the views of Church dissenters. Certainly somebody should speak up about this abuse. However, if a group attempts to question the policies of the diocesan newspaper, it may well find that priests favorably disposed to the group will feel they cannot join because it is criticizing a diocesan newspaper. In such circumstances, many priests might even fear reprisals if they were associated with such a group.

Once again the small-group concept solves the problem. Instead of having just one large group, there can be certain small groups that only promote the good while other small groups also speak out against abuses. As indicated earlier, these groups would communicate and work together on large projects while retaining their independence of operation.

HOW THE GROUPS MIGHT OPERATE

Here is one possible way that a group trying to promote Church doctrine might operate.

First, like the Vincent de Paul group, the members would be five or six in number. They would meet each week for a regular time but the meetings would be relatively short instead of dragging on for hours. In their meetings, the group would follow the policy of "see, judge, act". In other words, they would first attempt to observe what the particular problem was in their area, then judge what they could do to correct it, and finally devise some concrete action-steps that each member could undertake.

With respect to the structure of the meeting, it would involve both prayer and action.

The meeting would begin with a prayer. Here it is important to remember what was discussed earlier. People can have different styles of praying. Nevertheless, it should be possible for four or five people to agree on a prayer that all of them find meaningful. If desired, the prayers could be changed from meeting to meeting. One week the group could read a passage from the Bible. The next week they might pray the Rosary. The third week they might compose their own prayer, etc. Whatever was chosen, the prayer service should be an attempt on the part of all the members to offer their meeting to God and to seek His guidance.

Having prayed, the next part of the meeting would involve a quick period of study. A few pages might be read from a good book. Or an article could be distributed before the meeting and each member asked to read it in preparation. The study should not be lengthy but it ought to help the members of the group to advance in knowledge either of Church doctrine itself or of a particular problem existing within the Catholic community.

After prayer and study, the meeting would turn to the action steps. Here the group would consider what each member could do to support the

Pope and Church with respect to the previous week's project. Each member would have a chance to report on what he was able to accomplish. For instance, if the particular project the group had chosen was to write letters of encouragement to orthodox theologians who are working actively in support of Church doctrine, then each member might read or exchange a copy of the letter he or she had written since the last meeting.

The atmosphere of the meeting should not be "all business". Like the Vincent de Paul organization, the small group should provide moments to relax and have fun. People should enjoy coming to the meeting.

At the same time, each member should leave the meeting with a feeling that something definite has been accomplished. It has not been simply "all talk" or "all socializing".

With respect to the length of the meeting, it would probably be best if weekly meetings took only an hour or an hour-and-a-half. (When meetings begin to take longer, people may tend to stay away.) As your group begins its work, it is important to understand that you are not expected to solve the whole problem. Just do your best. The blunt truth is that the problem of dissent will probably afflict the Church for many, many years. Nevertheless, if each individual in your group regularly takes a specific action-step in support of Church teaching, you will be surprised at the tremendous results that can be achieved over a period of time.

A number of years ago Ripley's *Believe It Or Not* carried the following story. Suppose a murder took place at midnight, and only two people knew about it. If each of these two people told two other people every twelve minutes and if each person who heard about the murder also told two other people every twelve minutes, the entire world would know about the killing by morning.

The principle behind this example is that, if many people do a little bit of work on a regular basis, the cumulative effect can be enormous.

In summary, an effective group of orthodox Catholics will have to inform its members about the problem and then give each member something specific to do in support of the Pope and Church teaching.

WHO IS THE GROUP TRYING TO REACH?

In planning the activity of a small group, we should always keep in our minds whom we are trying to reach.

First, our efforts should be directed toward those who already agree with us. We need to show such Catholics that they are not alone. We must find these Catholics and then tell them what they can do—encourage them to become active themselves in support of the Pope and Church teaching and present them with specific examples of how they can do this.

The second group we are trying to reach are those Catholics who are unsure—those who could go one way or the other with respect to supporting the Pope and Catholic doctrine.

While we can be of much assistance to orthodox Catholics and unsure Catholics, we can probably do little with those who might be classified as the "firm dissenters". Barring a miracle of God's Grace, they will simply not be open to our activity. They have already made their choice. Far from encouraging what we are doing, they will do everything in their power to block us from being effective.

Because our goal is to reach out to other Catholics, the groups we form will have to be alert to a certain danger that can easily affect small groups—and that is the danger of talking only to ourselves. It is natural and right for us to associate with people who already share our experiences. To succeed in promoting Church doctrine, however, we must also become "missionaries" to other Catholics.

Yet there is a problem here. There is a sense in which those who are not already convinced cannot be in your group. Yet there is another sense in which they ought to be. Perhaps an example will illustrate the difficulty.

Suppose that you are committed to a certain political candidate. Let us call him Mr. Jones. Now the whole goal of your efforts is to reach out to other voters and to convince them to vote for Jones. Therefore, you want to come into frequent contact with anybody who might be a possible vote for Jones. You want to speak to those who are not as yet convinced. You want to develop projects that will bring the already convinced Jones supporters into close contact with those who might become Jones backers in the future.

At the same time, however, the Jones For Office group must necessarily consist of those already committed to Jones. After all, if a sizable number of those involved in a group that was started to promote Jones were not as yet convinced that they wanted to support him, then the whole purpose of the group would be thwarted.

What we are really saying is that there is a need for two different kinds of groups—or, if you will, two different kinds of activity. There is a need for one type of meeting in which the people already committed to Jones come together in order to plan a strategy that will increase support for Jones. Then there is a need for a second type of meeting in which those who want to learn more about Jones can come into contact with those already committed to him and will hopefully themselves become committed.

In other words, there is a need for a group that is missionary in nature and also a need for a group of those who are already committed.

If we reflect on it, we will see that the Church Herself faces the same problem. In the early Church, for instance, those who were learning about Christianity—those who were in the process of becoming converts—left after the first part of the Mass which was called the Mass of the Catechumens. Only those who were already committed stayed for the second part of the Mass—the Mass of the Faithful—in which they received the Body and Blood of the Lord. By such a procedure, the early Church was recognizing that there was a need for a kind of gathering that was directed towards those not yet ready to make a full commitment to Christ. This was the first part of the Mass with its emphasis on what Jesus had said and on the teaching of the Church. At the same time, the Church understood the need for a special gathering of those already committed to Christ. This was the Mass of the Faithful.

The small groups we have been talking about are for Catholics who are already committed to the Pope and Catholic doctrine. However, a major goal of the group is to increase support for Church teaching among other Catholics.

NEWCOMERS TO THE GROUP

Suppose that your group has been in existence for some time. Now you have found two other Catholics who, sharing your views about the Pope and Catholic teaching, would like to join the group.

This is a wonderful development. It is vital that the movement grow and this can only happen if new members are brought into the groups. At the same time, the addition of "newcomers" can present an unusual difficulty for the "veterans". As part of a training program, it will be necessary for the group to discuss in considerable detail a number of things that the more experienced members of the group already know.

Sometimes it is quite difficult for experienced people to do this. When you have become very familiar with a particular subject, there is often a tendency to speak in a kind of "short-hand"—to assume things that newcomers to the group may not know at all.

Therefore, as new members come into the group, the "veterans" must never show any impatience or lack of willingness to discuss what they themselves may have covered a long time before. Nor must there be any annoyance if others do not quickly understand what seems obvious to the veterans. That is all part of the learning process. With prayer and patience, the group will eventually be stronger than ever as the enthusiasm of the newcomers is added to the experience of the veterans.

Once formed, a small group should not stay within itself but should attempt to multiply. If there are six people in the group, perhaps a good goal would be to create a second group by the end of the year with three veterans from the original group joining with two or three new people. In this way each group would double within the course of a year.

"PUBLIC RELATIONS" ON BEHALF OF CHURCH DOCTRINE

In its work, each group should consciously try to act in the best way to promote the teaching of Christ.

Secular society talks of "marketing" or "public relations". In using these terms, I am tempted to say that the concept of "public relations" has a problem in public reactions. By this I mean that, when people use these terms, they usually think of something artificial.

It is somewhat like the word politics. Many of us, whenever we think of the word "politics", visualize somebody who is not sincere but who will promise us anything to get our vote. In the same way, when we think of marketing, we imagine a salesman who will do anything to get us to buy a product—a salesman who is not really interested in us but in selling us something for his own advantage. When we think of public relations, we visualize a slick advertising man who is interested in the image rather than in the reality.

However, when we speak of "public relations" in connection with promoting Church doctrine, we are thinking about something else. We are not talking about giving a surface glamour to something that actually has no true quality. We are not talking about tricking somebody into buying a product. Rather, we are referring to a situation where the "product" (if we can use that term) is excellent—namely, the Gospel of Christ Himself. What we are really talking about is how to present this Gospel in such a way that people will not be put off by what we do but will be attracted to Jesus.

DIFFERENT PERSONALITIES

All of us have had experience with different kinds of people. For instance, there is a certain type of individual that we might refer to as Jovial Jim. When talking to other people, Jovial Jim comes across as warm and friendly. Outside of their hearing, however, Jim is not interested in the other people at all. In fact, he makes disparaging remarks about them.

On the other hand, there is Shy Sarah. She is truly concerned about others but finds great difficulty in expressing it. Many people are like Sarah—unable to express their feelings. For instance, some parents love their children but find it almost impossible to tell them so.

Of course, there are outgoing personalities ("Jovial Jims") who are as sincere as the "Shy Sarahs". But these people usually do not need help in communicating with others. They are naturally talented in this regard. Here we are thinking of Catholics who want to promote Church doctrine but who may have problems in doing this successfully. In the spirit of Jesus Himself, these orthodox Catholics truly love those whom they are trying to bring to the Church's teaching. Somehow that love must be expressed in a way that advances Catholic doctrine. We who support the Pope must never seem to be reserved or withdrawn (or hostile or angry) because, if that is the way we appear, we will not be effective missionaries for Christ.

Therefore, we must pray for the ability to control any hostile feelings and constantly check ourselves to be sure that we are never blocking Christ. It is said that in the early Church many pagans were drawn to the new religion because they saw the actions of Christians and said to themselves: "See how these Christians love one another." Above all else that is the way we will bring others to orthodox Catholic teaching.

In closing this section, perhaps we should consider the example of groups such as the Jehovah's Witnesses. Many of us have had the experience of finding somebody from that group knocking at our door. On the one hand, their zeal is laudable. They have a willingness to be laughed at—they risk being scorned—in order to achieve what they consider good. That is the kind of sacrifice orthodox Catholics must be willing to make for the Pope and Church doctrine.

On the other hand, the Jehovah's Witnesses sometimes are so aggressive and pushy that they turn people off. Whenever people believe they are being forced into something, their emotions are aroused and it becomes very difficult for them to accept what is being said. Therefore, while still being as zealous as the Jehovah's Witnesses, we must try to avoid anything that produces a negative reaction.

Of course, even if we do avoid such aggressiveness, even if we act in the spirit of love, the dissenters will be upset. After all, if they ridicule the Pope, will they do anything less for us? However, there is all the difference in the world between people who get upset unjustly and people who get upset because we ourselves acted in the wrong way and created obstacles. Therefore, while we must never be afraid to act, we must pray unceasingly that our work will always be undertaken within the Spirit of Jesus Himself.

WHAT SPECIFICALLY TO DO

To this point, we have been discussing how a group might operate and stressing the importance of reaching out to others.

As we attempt to communicate with other Catholics, we should keep in mind that studies reveal that some people are affected most by what they read, while others are influenced principally by what they see or hear. Everyone, however, is affected by personal contact with other people. (After all, when we think about it, this is the way that mothers teach their children.) Therefore, in recognition of the way that people communicate, orthodox Catholics should be prepared to offer books and other reading material as well as tapes and visual presentations. Most of all, they should offer other Catholics opportunities to communicate on a personal level with those who support the Pope and Catholic doctrine.

Because of the importance of personal contact, the activity of the local group cannot be overemphasized. Previously I presented an example of the influence of the Right to Life movement. At that time we were considering the impact that parents who were active pro-life workers had upon their own children. Let us now present one other example from the pro-life movement that demonstrates the importance of local activity.

Before most people began to join pro-life groups, there was a period of time in which Catholics tended to leave this matter to the bishops. They thought that, since the Church was a large organization, the influence of the bishops would be sufficient to prevent pro-abortion legislation from passing in Congress or the state legislatures. On the other hand, while pro-life Catholics were leaving everything to their bishops, the pro-abortionists were forming groups and lobbying the legislators personally.

As long as this pattern prevailed, the pro-abortionists were gaining in the legislatures. However, when pro-life people realized that they personally had to become active—that it would not work to leave the matter to others, even to bishops—that their own action could have a major impact—that it was a serious mistake to imagine that one needed a large organization with a million dollars to be effective—in other words, when people began to do what they could, then the pro-life movement took great leaps forward.

That is the way it must be with the struggle to promote Church doctrine. Certainly we hope that those who exercise authority within the Church will always act vigorously for Church doctrine. However, it is a serious mistake to think that only Church authorities possess the ability to act effectively. Rather, all Catholics are called upon to work and promote Catholic teaching as best we can. Until many orthodox Catholics on the local level begin to speak out for the Pope, we will not have the progress that we should.

The basic reason for this is something we have just mentioned. People are influenced primarily by those within their own community with whom they come into personal contact. To the extent this is true, it means that not even the Pope can do what you are in a position to accomplish within your community. Why? Because you are physically present there while the Holy Father is not. That is the reason the dissenters invariably try to discourage any local initiative by loyal Catholics. Instinctively, they realize how devastating to them that kind of witness could be.

Although this is only a partial list, here are a few specific projects that a group wishing to promote Church teaching could undertake.

1) Set up a program in your own parish or community. Invite a speaker who is effective in defending the Pope and Church teaching. Do not be disappointed if only the already convinced come to the meeting because it is important to encourage these orthodox Catholics. If this happens, however, a later attempt should be made to reach out to the doubtful—going door-to-door if necessary.

If some members of your group have an influence within the local CCD or religious education program, the program could be put on there. If blocked in the CCD, perhaps it could be sponsored by a local parish society such as the Holy Name or Mothers' Club. If blocked even there, nobody can prevent you from inviting people to your own home to hear a speaker defend Church doctrine.

2) Compile a list of orthodox books and tapes that you find effective. Publicize them to others. For example, members of your group could give such books or tapes to friends as presents or encourage the local parish to place such materials in the pamphlet rack in the back of the Church or visit religious book stores and repeatedly request orthodox books and tapes in order to make sure that they are ordered by the store and placed on the shelves.

3) Write your own newsletter. In addition to promoting Church doctrine through books and tapes, there is a great need for newsletters in which groups who support the Pope can communicate with each other. This could be called "internal communication". A small group could prepare such a newsletter and distribute it to other orthodox Catholics.

4) Join with other groups in larger projects. For instance, orthodox groups might sponsor a march in support of the Pope or some other kind of rally to express backing for Church teachings—especially for teachings that are under attack by the dissenters. Such a large rally can be valuable for several reasons. First, it is a public expression of support for Church doctrine. Second, it can give inspiration and encouragement to those orthodox Catholics who participate. Third, it is an excellent way to educate those who may not be aware of the crisis within the Church or who are "on the fence". A rally of this kind provides the opportunity to feature a good speaker and display orthodox books and pamphlets.

5) Express public support for the Pope through advertisements in the newspapers—Catholic or secular. One type of advertisement could be a "signature ad" in which Catholics allow their names to be listed publicly in support of the Pope. Or the ad could be a well-written defense of Church teaching and an appeal to Catholics to back the Holy Father.

6) Write letters in support of Catholic doctrine:

A. LETTERS OF ENCOURAGEMENT

Letters of support should be written to those who are promoting Church doctrine (the Pope, orthodox theologians, faithful priests that you know on the local level, etc.). If someone has helped you, it is important to tell them. Such letters of encouragement are rarely received but they can be tremendously inspiring to those who have been working tirelessly in support of the Church's teaching.

B. LETTERS DEFENDING CATHOLIC DOCTRINE

Whenever a Church teaching is criticized in a secular or "Catholic" publication, one of the members of your group should write a letter defending the Church's doctrine.

Suppose that the problem is that your diocesan newspaper regularly publishes columns attacking Church teaching. In response, your group ought to write an article or a letter that defends the Church's position. The diocesan newspaper should be asked to publish it. (If the newspaper refuses to print your article or letter, and if they have not published an adequate defense of the Pope's view on this matter by some other orthodox Catholic, then the diocesan bishop and the Vatican itself should be informed.)

This process should be repeated on every occasion when the opinions of the dissenters are published by the diocesan newspaper. Some editors favorable to Church dissenters pretend that they have provided "balanced coverage" if they publish one orthodox article for every twelve dissenting articles. They should not be allowed to get away with such a maneuver.

In addition to letters that are intended for publication, personal letters should be written to the editors themselves. However, you should write not only to the editor but to the diocesan bishop and even to the Vatican.

In writing, emphasize the effect that the publication of dissent can have on the faith of Catholics. Be sure of your facts whenever you write because the dissenters will try to discredit you if they can find some factual mistake in what you have said. Therefore, it is important to document your statements whenever possible. For example, if you are writing to the Vatican about articles that appear in your diocesan newspaper, it is a good idea to send to the Vatican the actual articles.

In your letters, do not attack the motives of Church dissenters. The important thing is not their motives but what they are doing. What your letters should stress is the harm being done to the faith of many Catholics.

Often Church dissenters use the power they have on the local level to oppress orthodox spokesmen or materials. For instance, dissenters on the priests' personnel board in a diocese may seek to have an orthodox pastor removed from his post. Or an orthodox catechism that promotes Church doctrine may be banned in a particular diocese.

Whenever such situations develop, it is essential that loyal Catholics write a great many letters to the diocesan bishop and to the Vatican requesting an investigation. Finding as many Catholics as possible to write such letters can be an important project for your group. The letters should stress the merit of the orthodox programs (or the orthodox person) that is under fire from the dissenters. Such circumstances also provide the occasion to point out both to Church authorities and to the general public that the dissenters are not the advocates of "freedom" that they pretend to be. Should not people who want an orthodox catechism have freedom? Why are the dissenters—those who talk incessantly about "pluralism"—prohibiting Catholics from selecting an orthodox catechism of their choice? This kind of question must be raised on every possible occasion until the power of local dissenters to intimidate orthodox Catholics is checked.

We have been concentrating on letters to "Catholic" newspapers. Letters should also flow in to secular publications whenever they publish material promoting Church dissent. If the secular newspaper refuses to give "equal time" to the orthodox Catholic viewpoint, ways should be found to publicize this fact.

Similar opportunities should be sought on radio and television to defend the Pope and Catholic doctrine. Recently a group of dissenters expressed the view that the media is their best ally. Loyal Catholics must work to correct this and insist that all secular media present the "other side". (Of course, when an opportunity to respond is presented to orthodox Catholics, it is then essential to have a good spokesman available.)

If you and other orthodox Catholics are still not satisfied by the coverage of the secular media, you should not hesitate to make a phone call and request a personal meeting with the editor of the newspaper or the manager of the radio or television station. If none of this works, it might even be advisable (as Right to Life groups have done with abortion clinics) to picket the newspaper or television station in a peaceful way—especially if it has adopted policies that are contemptuous of Church teaching. I am convinced that, if the secular media began to encounter several hundred Catholics in front of their offices every time they attacked Catholic doctrine, their anti-Church policies might soon be softened. Even in such picketing, however, the spirit involved should not be one of hate but of standing up for the truth and expressing support for the Pope.

7) In addition to letters, seek every opportunity to meet with Church authorities to inform them of the problems faced by orthodox Catholics.

While most Catholics may not have realized it, the bishops of our country have for years permitted groups and individuals to meet with them in order to express opinions. Committees are set up for just this purpose. On the national level, groups can write to these committees of bishops and request a meeting. The dissenters are constantly doing this. For that reason alone, groups that support the Pope and Church doctrine should also communicate regularly with the bishops.

In meeting either with a group of bishops or with the bishop of a diocese, it is good to make specific requests. For instance, suppose your diocese is one of those that publishes a column which regularly criticizes the Pope or Church teaching. Now you are meeting with the diocesan bishop or his representative. In such a situation, one specific request to make of the bishop is that an orthodox columnist also appear in the newspaper every week so that Church doctrines can be promoted. (Of course, if the bishop were following the will of the Holy Father, the column by the dissenter would not appear at all. However, if your group cannot obtain this, you should request that a strong advocate of orthodox Catholic teaching be given regular access to the newspaper.)

One of the advantages of having many small groups instead of one large group is that each of the small organizations can request its own opportunity to meet with the bishop. On the other hand, if only a single large group of orthodox Catholics exists in the diocese, there may be only one occasion when the bishop hears the views of Catholics committed to support of the Pope.

In addition to talking to the bishops, orthodox Catholics should also talk as often as possible to pastors, to assistant pastors and, in fact, to anyone they can. Such conversations should take place not only on formal occasions but whenever informal opportunities present themselves. Our Lord's example of knocking at the door should always be before us.

Again I stress that these examples represent only a partial list of what Catholic groups can do. In its work, the group should make use of any particular talents and skills its members possess. Therefore, if some members are good speakers, they can be the spokesmen in public discussions. If others have experience in teaching, they can be the educators who suggest lists of suitable materials or who draw up a curriculum that parents can employ in explaining Catholic doctrine to their children. However, if your group has none of these particular talents, it is still important to try your best in all these areas. As the Gospels make clear, God can work beautifully even through those who do not seem to have special abilities. Therefore, if someone is naturally talented in writing a good letter, perhaps he or she can draft one for you (as long as it truly represents your views). But do not let this talented individual be the only one whose name appears on letters from your group. It is important for you and every other orthodox Catholic to write as many letters as possible and to take any other actions that will help to promote the Pope's teaching.

CONCLUSION: THE MAIN THEME OF THIS BOOK

A well known Church dissenter recently called on "more Catholics to think and debate and agitate beyond the party line". He was urging the dissenters to continue their activity and to expand their numbers. The main theme of this book is that exactly the same call must go out to orthodox Catholics. It is necessary for more and more of us to plan and to debate and to agitate and to work for the official Church teaching. Only in this way will orthodox Catholic doctrine be promoted as it should. The work cannot be left to others—even to Church authorities such as the bishops.

To use a sports example, it often seems that orthodox Catholics within the Church are like two outfielders on a baseball team. A ball is hit in their area. Either player could catch it, but each expects that the other player will act. So the ball drops untouched and the game is lost.

Groups of orthodox Catholics must stop expecting that other orthodox Catholics will do the job. Instead, they must do it themselves.

I might add that, unlike the sports example, where in fact only one player catches the ball, the task of promoting Church doctrine can be undertaken by many, many people and groups. If the bishops are doing their best, but lay people are also working in support of the Pope, this "double activity" does not hurt in any way. To the contrary, it adds an indispensable aspect to the effort to give witness to the Catholic faith. There simply cannot be "too many people" or "too many groups" working in support of Church teaching.

TWO SAINTS

As we consider the task that confronts orthodox Catholics in today's Church, let us go back hundreds, even thousands of years, and end this section with a quotation from two famous Church saints. Notice that their words, like many other statements from the past, are as relevant as if they had been written yesterday. For that reason, the Church has made both these quotations a part of the Divine Office that Her priests are expected to pray daily.

St. John Chrysostom, bishop of Constantinople, died in the year 407. Twice forced into exile by the hatred of the imperial court and the envy of his enemies, St. John had to suffer much for the Faith. In this passage, he reflects (commenting on that part of St. Matthew's Gospel in which Jesus tells His disciples: "I am sending you out like sheep among wolves. You must be clever as snakes and innocent as doves.") on the way that the followers of Christ should react to controversy and turmoil.

As long as we are sheep, we overcome and, though surrounded by countless wolves, we emerge victorious; but if we turn into wolves, we are overcome, for we lose the shepherd's help. He, after all, feeds the sheep not the wolves, and will abandon you if you do not let him show his power in you.

What he says is this: "Do not be upset that, as I send you out among the wolves, I bid you be as sheep and doves. I could have managed things quite differently and sent you, not to suffer evil nor to yield like sheep to the wolves, but to be fiercer than lions. But the way I have chosen is right. It will bring you greater praise and at the same time manifest my power." That is what he told Paul: *My grace is enough for you, for in weakness my power is made perfect.* "I intend", he says, "to deal in the same way with you." For, when he says, *I am sending you out like sheep,* he implies: "But do not therefore lose heart, for I know and am certain that no one will be able to overcome you."

The Lord, however, does want them to contribute something, lest everything seem to be the work of grace, and they seem to win their reward without deserving it. Therefore he adds: *You must be clever as snakes and innocent as doves.* But, they may object, what good is our cleverness amid so many dangers? How can we be clever when tossed about by so many waves? However great the cleverness of the sheep as he stands among the wolves—so many wolves!—what can it accomplish? However great the innocence of the dove, what good does it do him, with so many hawks swooping upon him? To all this I say: Cleverness and innocence admittedly do these irrational creatures no good, but they can help you greatly.

What cleverness is the Lord requiring here? The cleverness of a snake. A snake will surrender everything and will put up no great resistance even if its body is being cut in pieces, provided it can save its head. So you, the Lord is saying, must surrender everything but your faith: money, body, even life itself. For faith is the head and the root; keep that, and though you lose all else, you will get it back in abundance. The Lord therefore counseled the disciples to be not simply clever or innocent; rather he joined the two qualities so that they become a genuine virtue. He insisted on the cleverness of the snake so that deadly wounds might be avoided, and he insisted on the innocence of the dove so that revenge might not be taken on those who injure or lay traps for you. Cleverness is useless without innocence.

Do not believe that this precept is beyond your power. More than anyone else, the Lord knows the true natures of created things; he knows that moderation, not a fierce defense, beats back a fierce attack.

As it was in John Chrysostom's time, so it is today. While we do not judge them—for we leave that to God—the Church dissenters often attack the faith of orthodox Catholics with a vehemence and a bitterness that can well be compared to an attack of wolves on sheep. We must use all our cleverness and all our abilities to defend Catholic teaching from these onslaughts, but we must never turn into wolves ourselves in the process.

And what is our guide through all this? St. Thomas Becket tells us. Archbishop of Canterbury, he was martyred in 1170 by agents of Henry II because he defended the Catholic Church from the maneuvers of the English king. He says:

> There are a great many bishops in the Church, but would to God we were the zealous teachers and pastors that we promised to be at our consecration, and still make profession of being. The harvest is good and one reaper or even several would not suffice to gather all of it into the granary of the Lord. Yet the Roman Church remains the head of all the churches and the source of Catholic teaching. Of this there can be no doubt. Everyone knows that the keys of the kingdom of heaven were given to Peter. Upon his faith and teaching the whole fabric of the Church will continue to be built until we all reach full maturity in Christ and attain to unity in faith and knowledge of the Son of God.

> Of course many are needed to plant and many to water now that the faith has spread so far and the population become so great. Even in ancient times when the people of God had only one altar, many teachers were needed; how much more now for an assembly of nations which Lebanon itself could not provide with fuel for sacrifice, and which neither Lebanon nor the whole of Judea could supply with beasts of burnt offerings!! Nevertheless, no matter who plants or waters, God gives no harvest unless he himself assents to Peter's teaching. All important questions that arise among God's people are referred to the judgment of Peter in the person of the Roman Pontiff. Under him the ministers of Mother Church exercise the powers committed to them, each in his own sphere of responsibility.

Remember then how our fathers worked out their salvation; remember the sufferings through which the Church has grown, and the storms the ship of Peter has weathered because it has Christ on board. Remember how the crown was attained by those whose sufferings gave new radiance to their faith. The whole company of saints bears witness to the unfailing truth that without real effort no one wins the crown.

Appendix I.
Sample Letters Expressing Support for Church Teaching

Letters of Encouragement:
  to the Pope
  to orthodox Catholics

Letters Expressing Support for Church Teaching:
  to all the Priests of a Diocese

Ad Promoting the Teachings of the Pope

Letter Announcing a March

Letter to Bishops about Disciplinary Change: (Holydays)

Speaking Out Against Abuses:
  Problem 1 - Lectures Being Sponsored:
    Letter to Diocesan Newspaper
    Letter to Bishop
    Letter from Priest to Other Priests in Diocese
  Problem 2 - Pastor and Altar Rail:
    Letter to Diocesan Newspaper
  Problem 3 - Diocesan Family Life Department Claims
  Contraception, Masturbation, and Homosexuality
  Can Be Justified at Times as Being In Accord
  with Church Teaching
  Problem 4 - Diocesan Newspaper Published Columns
  of Dissenters:
    Letter to Bishop Requesting Meeting

    This appendix contains an illustration of the kinds of letters that orthodox Catholics could write in support of Church teaching. Although each letter covers a somewhat different situation, the ideas presented are similar and, for that reason, there will be some repetition. However, groups supporting Church doctrine should realize that repetition is something we will have to do. Like an advertiser, we will have to repeat the same themes over and over again—perhaps hundreds of times. For instance, it is not good enough to say only once that Church dissenters do not speak for "American Catholics". Since the dissenters make this claim repeatedly, we must deny it just as repeatedly.

These samples are presented as guides that your group may wish to use in writing your own letters. After some of the letters, a few comments are added.

A. LETTERS OF ENCOURAGEMENT

Example 1:

Recalling how Pope Paul VI told Bishop Sheen (see Book II) that virtually every letter the Holy Father received contained a thorn, we should not hesitate to write to the Pope himself. This letter is intended to be not a thorn but a sincere thank-you to the Pope for his efforts in support of Catholic teaching.

Sample Letter:

Your Holiness,

Recently I read stories in both *Time* and *Newsweek* that tried to give the impression that "American Catholics" oppose what you are doing to emphasize the Church's doctrine. The articles—like many that appear in the press—suggested that the Pope does not understand "American Catholics".

I am an American Catholic. My purpose in writing is to say how much I support your actions. I believe with all my heart in the teachings of the Catholic Church. Like many other Catholics, I have suffered when Catholic doctrine is ridiculed by some who claim to be Catholic theologians.

In this situation, many Catholics have become confused. Some have even been tempted to abandon their faith. It is to people such as these that you speak when you stress Church doctrine as you have been doing.

At times, many of us who support you are silent. (There is, unfortunately, a tendency for people not to write when they agree. Only those who dissent write.) Nevertheless, I hope you will always know that we are there, and that we cherish and believe in *all* (not just some) of the teachings of our Church.

Thanking you for your spiritual leadership, I am

Respectfully yours,
(name)

Example 2:

A letter that might be sent to an orthodox theologian often under attack from Church dissenters.

Sample Letter:

Dear Father Jones,

This letter is simply a thank you for the wonderful work that you are doing. When you speak out on behalf of the official teaching of the Church, you confirm a great many of us in our faith. You will probably never know how many Catholics you have helped.

I realize that you have made great sacrifices to speak out for the Church's teaching. In the topsy-turvy world of the present, theologians like yourself are banned from certain dioceses while Church dissenters are welcomed. The vicious treatment you receive must often make you feel discouraged. But still you persevere in Christ's work!

Thanking you again with all my heart for your support of the Pope and for teaching us Catholic doctrine, I am

Respectfully yours,
(name)

B. LETTER EXPRESSING SUPPORT FOR CHURCH TEACHING

Dear Father:

This letter is being sent to all the priests of the Diocese. Its purpose is to inform you about our group, a newly formed organization called the *Committee to Promote the Doctrinal Teaching of the Holy Father*. We would like to invite you to participate in our program, if you agree with our goals.

Our goal is to promote the official teaching of the Catholic Church. We believe it is especially important to do this in the present age when not only from without but even from within many Church teachings are being challenged.

In describing our Committee perhaps the first thing to do is to explain what we are not.

First, we are not a group that will criticize any official parish program or diocesan program that currently exists within the Diocese. *We are interested solely in promoting the official teaching set forth by our Holy Father.*

Second, we will not be concerned with areas in which the Church itself allows options, but solely with areas in which the Pope has made a decision that he intends to be binding on the Church.

Finally, in inviting you to take part in our program, we will not be using your name without your permission.

Let me explain each of these in turn.

With respect to the first statement, we know that there are groups that have expressed concern about official programs in which views are put forth that are contrary to Church teaching. However, we realize that, if we were to do this, it would make it very difficult for many Diocesan priests to take part in our program. Even if a priest fully supported the Pope's teaching, he might hesitate to join a group that publicly criticized anything going on in the Diocese. Therefore, we will not make any such statements. We are solely concerned with the answer to these questions: *"What can we Catholics do to promote the teachings of the Holy Father? How can we take these teachings and encourage others to listen to what the Pope is saying?"*

Second, we will not take a stand on any question where the Church itself permits an option. In other words, we will not attempt to "be more Catholic than the Pope". For instance, the Church itself permits a choice as to whether Communion should be received in the hand or on the tongue—so that would not be an area in which we are concerned. Nor will we be involved with questions of Church finances or personnel—important as these areas may be.

As our name indicates, what we are concerned about is, above all, the doctrinal teaching set forth by our Holy Father. However, we are also concerned about any binding decisions the Pope may have made with respect to matters that might be called disciplinary rather than doctrinal. For instance, it is our understanding that the Vatican believes the normal policy should be first Penance to precede first Communion. Since this is a decision that has been made by the Pope which he wants the Church to carry out, such an issue would fall in the area in which our Committee hopes to work.

Finally, if you choose to take part in the program that we will be presenting in the next few paragraphs, we assure you that your name will never be used without your permission. Nor will you have to attend any meetings. Instead, what we are seeking is a sharing of ideas. We hope you will give us your thoughts on how best to promote the teachings of the Holy Father.

Now that we have explained what we are not, let us discuss what we hope to do. We want to begin a discussion among those Catholics in the Diocese who are fully in support of the Pope's teaching. How can we work together to assist the Pope in the present doctrinal crisis?

If you are interested in taking part in our program and receiving our mailings, please return the enclosed blue sheet of paper. It lists your name and address. Once we have received it, we will put you on the list to receive all subsequent information.

You will note that we also request you to send us the names of any lay people and any religious that you believe would be interested in taking part in this discussion. As with your name, these names will not be given out to anyone. They will simply provide us with a mailing list to whom we can distribute the materials that we are asking you yourself to take part in devising.

On the blue sheet, we also ask you to indicate whether you support all the official teachings of the Pope—even controversial teachings such as *Humanae Vitae*. We do this because we would like to be able to prove that there are many priests who agree with the position of the Holy Father. Often both those challenging the Pope and the secular media give exactly the opposite impression, the impression that virtually nobody in the United States supports the views of the Pope, at least on the so-called "controversial" teachings.

As one example, *Newsweek* recently published an article entitled "The Pope Vs. the U.S. Church". The article began as follows: "What has Pope John Paul II got against American Catholics and their Church? A number of U.S. bishops, just back from a month of meetings with the Pope, are troubled by that question. So are thousands of American priests, nuns and seminary educators—and for good reasons."

Newsweek goes on to explain that what disturbs these "Americans" is the Pope's emphasis on certain Catholic doctrines. As one example, *Newsweek* mentions artificial contraception, a teaching that *Newsweek* says "American Catholics" reject. So, in making such statements the Pope is opposing "American Catholics".

As part of its propaganda campaign against the Pope, *Newsweek* deliberately creates the impression that any American Catholics who might support the Pope are few in number and insignificant.

Now we think this is wrong. In fact, it is garbage—and with your help, we can prove it.

Therefore, while we will not use your individual name without your permission, we hope you will take this opportunity to "vote for the Pope's teachings" by expressing your support for his views.

But what about those priests who dissent from at least some teachings of the Church? While we are not questioning their sincerity, it would seem to be very difficult for them to take part in a group that seeks to promote teachings they themselves do not believe in. Nevertheless, if you consider yourself in this category, but would still like to receive information, please so indicate by checking the second statement on the blue sheet and returning your name to us.

From what we have just written, we are sure some priests will agree with us while others will not. If you agree, we hope you will join our effort to share ideas with other priests and lay people who feel this same way.

We've now explained the first sheet. But, as you will note, there is also a second sheet. Here is where we ask you to write down your own thoughts on what Catholics can do to promote the Pope's teaching.

It is possible that this second sheet, which is on red paper, may take you more time than the first sheet. If this is the case, we ask you to return the first sheet now and send us the second sheet when you have time to write down your thoughts. You can also send us some of your views now and add additional thoughts later.

Of course, the question *"What can Catholics do to promote the Pope's teaching?"* is such a big question that many, many pages could be written on it. If you choose to participate in this exchange of ideas, you are welcome to write as little or as much as you wish.

(For example, one possible way to respond to this question would be to list the books, magazines, cassettes, and other materials that you have found helpful in promoting the teachings of the Holy Father. Many lay people would be very appreciative of such a list. Another way to respond would be to give some specific suggestions as to what a group of five or ten Catholics could do if they wish to express their support for the official teaching of the Church.)

As we have already indicated, we will not publish your name unless you yourself tell us to. If you share your ideas with us, it is our intention then to photocopy what you have said and to mail it to everyone else on our mailing list—that is, all those who have indicated a desire to discuss how best we can promote the teachings of the Holy Father. However, we will not be including your name when we distribute what you have written to the other priests unless you specifically tell us to do so. The reason for this is that we want to preserve the confidentiality of your thoughts at all times.

When you receive the written comments of others, you might wish to write something further about what they have said. This will then be distributed in a later mailing to all those on our list.

What do we hope to accomplish? Two things. First, by sharing ideas, we can learn from each other. Some of you probably have ideas about what we can do to promote the teaching of the Pope that others may never have thought of. This is a way to distribute such ideas. Second, and equally important, it will demonstrate that Catholics who want to promote the Pope's teachings are by no means a small group. Sometimes we can feel alone and isolated. It seems to us this often happens because we have not attempted to communicate with each other. While respecting the confidentiality of everyone involved, this program hopes to provide such communication.

What we have just outlined is an experimental program. We believe it can work if there are enough priests and lay people willing to take part in it. If you support our goals, we hope you will assist us by—first, returning your name so that you can be on our mailing list and—

second, by sharing your thoughts with us on how we can work for the doctrinal teaching of the Pope.

Thank you for any help you can give to us. On behalf of the committee, we remain,

Sincerely yours,
(name)

(Emphasis provided as on original letter.)

(BLUE)

Committee to Promote

the Doctrinal Teaching

of

the Holy Father

RESPONSE SHEET

NAME:_____
ADDRESS:_____
_____

Please check appropriate box and, if possible, return by: 12-31-83

☐ I believe in and support all the official doctrinal teachings of the Holy Father, including those that are often challenged today (e.g., *Humanae Vitae*). I want to promote these teachings and I am interested in hearing the views of other Catholics with similar convictions as to how we can best support the Pope.

☐ I do not believe in and support all the official doctrinal teachings of the Church (e.g., *Humanae Vitae*). Nevertheless, I would still like to receive your mailings.

NOTE: This initial mailing is being sent to all the priests of the Diocese. However, we would also like to communicate with any sisters, brothers or lay people who are committed to all the Church's teachings and who would like to do what they could to promote them.

If you know of any such individuals who would be interested in this effort, please list their names and addresses below:

(RED)

Committee to Promote

the Doctrinal Teaching

of

the Holy Father

HOW CAN WE PROMOTE THE POPE'S TEACHING?

Please take as much space, and additional paper as you wish to discuss this general question:

IN AN AGE WHEN DISSENT IS SO PROMINENT, WHAT CAN CATHOLICS DO TO EXPRESS SUPPORT FOR THE POPE AND TO PROMOTE THE OFFICIAL TEACHING OF THE CHURCH?

(This sheet can be returned either with the response sheet or at a later time.)

Comments:

This letter was actually sent to the priests of a particular diocese. Note that it contains many of the features that we previously discussed.

First, the group decided only to promote Church doctrine rather than criticize diocesan programs that were sympathetic to Church dissenters. As the letter indicates, this decision was made in order to make it easier for orthodox priests to associate with the group. As another way to make these priests feel more comfortable, the letter emphasized that the names of those who responded would always be kept secret.

The letter represents a first attempt to build up a list of those orthodox Catholics who believe strongly that the Pope should be supported. In this regard, it asks the priests not only to respond personally but to send in the names of lay people who also want to act in defense of the Holy Father.

Two other aspects of the letter should also be noted. First, the group chose to concentrate on doctrinal matters (and on the need to obey the current Church discipline) rather than express any views on whether changes in Church discipline would be desirable. Second, in addition to compiling a list of persons, the letter represents an attempt to compile a list of orthodox materials. The priests are asked to recommend books and articles that other orthodox Catholics might find helpful.

Despite its care, any group undertaking such a task should expect to be attacked. In fact, this was the case. One priest sympathetic to Church dissenters responded by tearing up the letter into little pieces. He sent it back with the sarcastic comment that he was forming a committee to suppress "ecclesiastical vigilantes". Another priest wrote that the letter might actually be the work of "the Communists". This priest, an advocate of theological dissent, was a prominent member of the diocesan priests' personnel board and had recently played a leading role in removing three orthodox pastors from their parishes and replacing them with "pastoral" priests who would tolerate dissent.

Yet a third dissenting priest attempted to dismiss the whole project by pointing out rather snobbishly that the laymen involved did not have post-graduate degrees in theology.

A final argument used by the dissenting priests was truly remarkable. Although they themselves were champions of dissent, they argued that the orthodox group was acting improperly because it had not sought permission of the local bishop before sending out its letter promoting Church doctrine. In this particular case, the dissenters knew that the bishop had long ago decided that the best policy with respect to doctrinal dissent was to "look the other way" and pretend it did not exist. Therefore, the bishop himself would not send such a letter and, if the dissenters could convince orthodox Catholics that approval by the bishop was required before anybody else could write, then no such project would ever be started.

In addition to this claim of Church dissenters that Catholics have no right to promote Church doctrine without the authorization of the bishop, a similar question is sometimes raised by orthodox Catholics themselves. For instance, one orthodox group was recently considering the idea of organizing a march in support of the Pope in their city. At that point, the question arose: Ought we to get permission from the local bishop?

To answer this question, let us first consider what Catholics are obliged to do and then what they might wish to do.

A good indication of the Church's own position on this subject can be found by looking at her present rules with respect to the publication of books that present Catholic doctrine. The Church requires that permission to publish be obtained from Church authorities only in circumstances where such works will be used in educational institutions or programs of catechetical instruction.

In saying this, it should be emphasized that all Catholics are morally obligated to follow the teaching of the Church in the books that they publish. Therefore, no Catholic has the right to publish a book that dissents from the Church's teaching. Here, however, we are not thinking of this but of the requirements set up by the Church itself for doctrinal works that are assumed to be orthodox. The present discipline of the Church is that such works must have Church approval if they are going to be used in official Church programs of religious education.

This rule of the Church with respect to books is a good guide to apply with respect to all other efforts to promote Church doctrine. Permission of the local bishop need not be obtained unless a group wishes to claim that the official Church is sponsoring or endorsing the project. Therefore, orthodox Catholics do not have to obtain the permission of the local bishop before arranging a march in support of the Pope—just as they do not have to obtain the permission of the local bishop before writing a letter to a newspaper in defense of the Pope.

As additional evidence that this position is correct, consider the attitude of the Vatican with respect to those groups in the United States that are known for their strong support of orthodox Catholic doctrine.

These are the very groups that are attacked as "fundamentalists" by those bishops who seem to be sympathetic to the dissenters. Yet Rome welcomes their efforts and key Vatican Cardinals, when visiting the United States, have gone out of their way to praise these groups and meet with their leaders. Obviously the Vatican Cardinals would not be acting in this way if the Pope disapproved of the activities of these orthodox organizations. Yet the groups involved clearly do not have the endorsement of the local bishop—at least in those dioceses where the bishop appears sympathetic to the dissenters.

To return to the case presented above, the dissidents were wrong in charging that the group of orthodox Catholics required the bishop's approval in order to write a letter asking for suggestions on the best way to promote Church teaching. Since the letter makes it clear that the effort is not an official project of the diocese, there is no obligation whatever to seek permission.

Having answered the question as to what loyal Catholics are required to do, let us now consider what they should do.

If you are scheduling a march for the Pope or some other project supporting Church doctrine, is it a good idea to obtain the permission of the local bishop?

Basically, it depends on the particular situation in your diocese. If you are in a diocese where the influence of the dissenters is so strong that the permission of the bishop would probably never be granted, then you should not hesitate to plan and execute such projects without seeking approval. After all, there is no obligation to request permission and the dissenters should not be given a veto power over your efforts to back the Pope.

The frustration of the dissenters at the letter from the Committee to Promote the Doctrinal Teaching of the Holy Father was largely caused by the fact that, as opposed to their ability to silence orthodox priests, the dissenters could do relatively little or nothing to the lay people who wrote the letter. For that reason, it is an excellent idea for lay people to lead such projects in dioceses where the dissenters are strong.

On the other hand, if you are in an area where orthodox groups have excellent relations with the bishop, then you may wish to inform him of what you are doing. If the bishop requests you to postpone a certain project and you know that the request is not an attempt to stifle such efforts but comes from a bishop who sides totally with the Holy Father, then the group should probably follow his wishes.

Even in such a situation, however, informing the bishop is not the same thing as requesting his permission. Often the bishop himself may not want to be put in such a position, especially with what is supposed to be a spontaneous project from "grass roots" Catholics. In general, therefore, it is probably best to inform sympathetic Church authorities about your upcoming projects—to ask for and welcome their assistance—but not to formally request permission. By such a procedure, you give the bishop the freedom to do whatever he wishes—to join with you in the project, to ask your group to change its plans, or to take no position at all.

To return to the sample letter from the group seeking to support the Holy Father, we have been considering the hostile reaction of Church dissenters. Their sharp and angry response shows us how deeply worried they are about the efforts of such groups.

What about the replies from orthodox priests? While the letter received many good and warm responses, a later investigation revealed that a number of other loyal priests did not return their names because they were afraid of the power of Church dissenters within their diocese. Despite the assurances that their names would remain secret, they were concerned that the dissenters would somehow be able to get the list. Then they would be punished. Sadly, this illustrates the terror that exists today in the hearts of many orthodox priests.

C. SAMPLE AD IN CATHOLIC NEWSPAPER PROMOTING THE TEACHINGS OF THE POPE

(Title) — *LET'S STAND UP PUBLICLY FOR THE POPE*

This ad is an appeal for your help in supporting our Holy Father. At present an organized effort is being made to create the false impression that "American Catholics" oppose the Pope's teachings on many important subjects. The Catholics whose names are listed below wish to go on public record in support of the Pope. We believe that he is the Vicar of Christ on earth. For that reason, we support *all* of his teachings on faith and morals.

(The rest of the page would consist of a list of names. At the bottom of the ad, the address of the group would be given and any Catholics who might read the advertisement would be invited to send in their names.)

Comment:

The example presented is a "signature ad" with a short text so as to leave space for as many Catholics as possible to list their names publicly in support of the Pope.

A second type of effective ad is the "text ad". For example, a text ad might explain in considerable detail how orthodox Catholics can form groups to promote Church doctrine.

D. SAMPLE LETTER ANNOUNCING A MARCH IN SUPPORT OF THE POPE

The following letter could be sent to individual Catholics or even inserted in a Church or secular newspaper as an advertisement:

Dear Fellow Catholic,

Today, unfortunately, there are some Catholics who are speaking out strongly against certain Church teachings. They also criticize the Holy Father when he urges Catholics to be faithful to these teachings.

Sometimes the public impression is created that all Catholics feel this way—that those who back the Pope are few and far between.

To demonstrate support for the Pope and for the Church's teaching, our group is organizing a public Rally and March. It will be held at (here insert details of time and place.)

At our March for the Pope, we will have the honor of being addressed by Fr. Edward Jones, a nationally known orthodox Catholic theologian. He and other speakers will outline additional steps that we may take to express our backing of the Holy Father.

As a symbol of our personal fidelity to the Holy Father and to Catholic doctrine, we are suggesting that each person coming to the March bring a red rose. The roses will be collected and placed in a floral arrangement to the right of the speaker's stand. The reason for this "rose project" is our belief that a great number of roses can be a visible way to demonstrate that there are countless numbers of Catholics who love the Church's teaching. (If you know of such a Catholic who cannot attend the March, you may wish to bring an additional rose as a sign of that Catholic's support.)

Hoping that you can assist us in making this March for the Pope a success, we are

Sincerely yours,
(Name of Organizing Committee)

E. LETTER ABOUT PROPOSED CHANGE IN CHURCH DISCIPLINE
(Elimination of holydays)

Dear Bishop:

I am writing this letter to you because I have heard there will be a proposal at the next Bishop's Meeting to abolish some of the Holy Days of Obligation.

Some years back a similar question was raised about the Holy Days and the bishops decided to poll some of the Catholic laity before making their decision. In a number of cities, people were allowed to vote after Sunday Mass on the question of whether to keep the Holy Days. When they were consulted in this way, the laity voted to keep all of them.

I realize that the Church is not a democracy. Nevertheless, I still feel that it was very helpful to give us a chance to express our views, especially since the question was not one of faith or morals. Instead, the question was whether a change would help us in our religious practice.

Since a precedent has been set to consult the laity on this matter, would it be possible to have a similar consultation before any decision is made this time? Otherwise, it could look as if, when we expressed our opinion last time, all that happened was that those who favored the proposal waited a number of years before pushing it again, this time being sure not to give the laity an opportunity to express their views.

Again, I recognize that it is not necessary to consult us. I also realize there may be people on the committee that formulated this proposal who are very much in favor of eliminating the Holy Days. It would probably mean delaying the decision for at least a few months, but I do not believe this kind of decision has to be made so quickly that a consultation with the laity is impossible.

Thank you for listening to my views.

Sincerely yours,
(name)

Comment:

A similar letter was actually sent to the bishops. In the real situation, a liturgical committee was pushing to eliminate several Holy Days of Obligation despite indications that many lay people desired to retain the existing Church law.

The letter concentrates on the importance of asking lay people for their opinion rather than on the merits of the question itself—whether a reduction in Holy Days would be desirable. This does not indicate that arguments with respect to the merits are unimportant. They are, in fact, the principal ones. However, the person writing the letter knew that other Catholics were writing to the Bishops about the merits and that those Bishops who agreed with their position were already committed in support of the present Holy Days. Since the vote by the Bishops was expected to be close, this letter attempted to appeal to those bishops who might not have been influenced by the discussion on the merits but who would respond favorably to the legitimate argument that no change ought to be made without consulting the laity—especially in a situation where a previous consultation with the laity had discovered that they did not want this change to be made.

F. SPEAKING OUT AGAINST ABUSES

While mentioning the problem of dissent, the previous sample letters and advertisements do not identify any specific activities of the dissenters but concentrate instead on urging Catholics to voice their support for the

Holy Father and Church doctrine. Here are a few letters that attempt to "fight the bad" by speaking out against the abuses of the dissenters.

Problem 1:

In your diocese only dissenting theologians have been invited to speak at a special "theological program" that is being held to "update" all Catholics. The program is sponsored by the diocesan seminary and the diocesan religious education program. Furthermore, the bishop has written to all of the priests of the diocese and has made attendance at this program compulsory. (These are not mere imaginings. Such abuses have in fact occurred in certain dioceses.)

Sample Letter to Diocesan Newspaper:

(Note: With adaption, this could also be a letter to a secular newspaper or an advertisement in the form of an open letter from concerned Catholics.)

Dear Editor,

Our diocesan newspaper recently carried a notice that our seminary was sponsoring a series of lectures by prominent theologians. Furthermore, it is my understanding that attendance by all the priests of the diocese has been made mandatory. Among the theologians invited to lecture the priests on Catholic doctrine are (list names).

Is it not true that the overwhelming majority of these invited theologians (perhaps all) have been and continue to be public dissenters to the official teaching of the Catholic Church on certain matters of faith and morals? For example, does even one of the invited theologians support *Humanae Vitae*?

In contrast to the theologians invited by our seminary, there are many other theologians who support *all* the teachings of the Church—not just some. There are theologians who have been outspoken defenders of the Holy Father's position on disputed doctrines such as *Humanae Vitae*. Yet none of these theologians has been invited!

Suppose another set of lectures were being given on political matters—but that all the speakers were liberal Democrats, while no Republican was allowed to participate. In such a circumstance, would not people rightly suspect that the lectures actually amounted to propa-

ganda for one particular side? Does not the announced series of "theological" lectures amount to the same thing? Vocal critics of the Pope are
welcomed with open arms—while vocal defenders of the Pope are left
out completely. Why?

(Signature of person sending letter)

Comment:

A letter very similar to the one above was in fact sent to one diocesan
newspaper. Although it was printed, the strategy chosen by the dissenters
was to ignore it completely, apparently because the letter concentrated on
the "fairness" question and the dissenters really had no way to respond
effectively. To combat this strategy of silence, it may be necessary for
orthodox Catholics to keep on sending letters until the dissenters feel
compelled to respond or until the general Catholic public becomes firmly
convinced that the "theological series" is propaganda.

In stressing that the dissenters are preventing a fair discussion by
banning orthodox theologians, the letter is trying to present an effective
argument to those Catholics who are "on the fence". Since these people
are not certain of their own position, they are unlikely to be impressed by
the argument that dissenters to the Pope should not be allowed to speak
(although that argument is in fact correct). However, they should be
influenced by the argument that they have been denied the opportunity to
hear orthodox Catholic theologians defend the Pope's view. As indicated
earlier, in those discussions where effective orthodox theologians are
allowed to participate, they usually do an excellent job in refuting the
claims of the dissenters (which is the very reason that the supporters of
dissent try to ban them).

Similar letters should be written every time a situation develops in
which a parish or diocese bans orthodox speakers or orthodox materials.

Finally, we might consider for a moment the obligation of Catholics
to attend such programs even if ordered to do so by the diocesan bishop or
other Church authorities. For instance, if the bishop orders all his priests
to attend lectures by theological dissenters, are they obliged to go? If a
parish priest requires an engaged couple to participate in a Cana Program
dominated by Church dissenters, are they obligated to go?

The first and most basic rule is that Catholics should never enter what
can be an occasion of sin. This rule takes precedence over any command

by the bishop or by parish to listen to Church dissidents. Thus, in the examples given, neither the priests nor the engaged couple is obligated to attend such programs and they should definitely stay away if they believe the program would in any way endanger their faith.

A similar question sometimes faces orthodox Catholics with respect to their own parishes. Suppose you live in a parish where those who dissent from the Pope's teachings have a great amount of influence. Not far away, however, there is another Catholic parish that is completely orthodox.

Normally, you should attend the parish where you live. Even if there was a Church rule to this effect, however, it would not bind you in your situation. Why? Because such a rule assumes that your parish is orthodox. It is not meant to apply to situations where the parish promotes the view of dissenters. Thus, Catholics should consider themselves free to choose another parish if their choice is motivated by the desire to find a local Catholic Church where orthodox teaching is promoted.

Although Catholics should not attend programs influenced by dissenters if they believe such programs could lead them to doubt Church teachings, it can also happen that orthodox Catholics will judge that their own faith is in no danger. Then they may decide that the best way to serve the Church is to attend such meetings and speak up for the Pope's position. Thus, in the examples given above, orthodox priests might decide to go to the lecture and orthodox Catholics might decide to remain in their parish in order to have somebody present in these places who will voice their support for the official Church teaching.

At times loyal Catholics may not know whether a program is dominated by Church dissenters until they have attended it. Thus, a Catholic couple may have no way of learning in advance whether a Cana Program will be an orthodox one or a program where views of the dissenters will be propagated. If the latter is the case, then, even though the program is now over, they should write to the diocesan bishop and to the Vatican recounting the events that took place and requesting that Church dissenters not be given such opportunities in the future.

Sample Letter to the Bishop of the Diocese:

Your Excellency,

I am writing this letter to express my concern about the series of lectures being sponsored by the diocesan seminary. Only theologians who oppose certain Church teachings have been invited and all priests of the diocese have been ordered to attend.

I know you yourself have stated that you support the Church teachings that these theologians deny. Despite your personal statements, however, is it not inevitable that such a program will have the effect of promoting the views of those who dissent from the Pope?

At the very least, should there not be a program where theologians who support these Church teachings are allowed to speak to the people of our diocese.

I write this not simply to raise an academic question. I know of many Catholics who are struggling to preserve their faith. How easy it is for them to become disillusioned and to abandon their faith when they see Catholic teaching being attacked by the very theologians who ought to be defending it.

Respectfully yours,
(Name of person sending letter)

Comment:

In addition to the bishop, the Vatican should be sent a copy of all such letters. If a response comes back from the bishop, a second letter should be written to him commenting on the response. If no response is received, then another letter requesting action should be sent to the bishop. If the bishop still does not respond, the Vatican should be so informed.

To whom should we write in the Vatican? To the Holy Father personally and to the heads of the Vatican Congregations that have responsibility over the particular areas in question (e.g., religious education and seminaries). The names and addresses of the Cardinals who head these Congregations can usually be found by consulting the National Catholic Almanac for the year in which you are writing.

If such letters are sent continually by increasing numbers of people, they will not only demonstrate to the Holy Father that great numbers of Catholics in the diocese support the Church's teaching, but they will also bring to the attention of the diocesan bishop (and of the Vatican) what is going on in the diocese.

Sample Letter to Priests of Diocese:

Dear Father,

This is a letter from some of your fellow diocesan priests. We wish to express our concern about the series of theological lectures being sponsored by the Diocesan Seminary. There are two reasons for our concern. First, these lectures highlight the views of Church dissenters while denying supporters of the Pope's position any representation. Second, attendance at these lectures will apparently be mandatory.

With respect to the first of these problems, we do not understand why those who dissent from the Pope are officially sponsored by our Diocese. Sometimes the argument is raised that it is necessary to have dialogue. But, if dialogue were really wanted, then why are defenders of the Pope excluded? Second, making such lectures mandatory for Diocesan priests amounts to treating us as if we were little children. Isn't it true that what is actually being said is the following: "We know you priests might choose not to attend if it were left to you—but we know best so we will order you children to be present."

When the Pope visited America a few years ago, he passed right through our Diocese and spoke only a short distance away. Yet there was no mandate ordering the priests of our Diocese to go and listen to the Pope. Ironically, such a mandate is only issued to the priests of our Diocese when the talks are given by those who dissent from the Pope.

Even if the proposed Diocesan program were the best one in the world, it should not be made obligatory for priests. Therefore, we hope that you will join us in urging that the mandatory aspects of the program be dropped. We also hope you will join us in asking why those who support the official teaching of the Church are not included in the program being offered.

Comments:

Fearing reprisals, orthodox priests may be reluctant to sign letters such as the one printed above, even though they approve of its contents. Under these circumstances, the letter should still be sent but without giving specific names.

A letter similar to this one was in fact sent to all the priests of a particular diocese. It had a definite impact. As a personal appeal from some unidentified priests to their colleagues, it was widely read. Since there was no possibility of eliminating the program being set up by the dissenters, the letter concentrated on reducing the program's impact by making it optional instead of mandatory. Because of the letter, many priests (even including a few sympathetic to the dissenters) began to urge that the program not be mandatory. As a result, those organizing it backed away from the attempt to require compulsory attendance.

Problem 2:

This is a situation that actually arose in a diocese where the influence of the dissenters was strong. The priests' personnel board attempted to remove an orthodox pastor from his parish. Although the pastor's emphasis on loyalty to the Pope was the principal consideration that led the dissenters to move against him, there were several other charges raised against him—including the interesting accusation that he had not taken down the altar rail in his parish. The dissenters felt that, in a "modern" church, Catholics should stand, rather than kneel, when receiving Holy Communion, and the presence of the altar rail would encourage kneeling.

When a secular newspaper reported that the failure to remove his parish altar rail was one of the reasons that the pastor had become "controversial", a letter similar to the following was sent to the diocesan newspaper.

Sample Letter to Diocesan Newspaper:

Dear Editor,

I have just read an article in *The Times* which reports on a shocking abuse that has been discovered in our Diocese. Do you know that not far from where you live there is actually a Catholic Church with an altar rail and that people kneel to receive Holy Communion?

Horrors! No wonder that the priests' personnel board sought to remove the pastor of that parish!

Some of us have been wondering why those who publicly dissent from Church teaching are left untouched by this same personnel board. Such dissenting priests continue to be pastors of parishes and little or nothing is ever done.

But, now that I have learned about the parish with the altar rail, I can understand the reason for the lack of action with respect to Church dissenters. After all, it is a question of priorities. The priests' personnel board must devote all its resources to fighting the most important battle of all—to make sure there are no altar rails left standing in our Diocese. Next to that, someone who denies the Real Presence of Christ in the Eucharist or questions the Divinity of Our Lord is obviously only a secondary problem.

Catholics kneeling to receive Holy Communion! What will they think of next?

Comment:

Humor and irony can be very effective weapons if challenging the activities of the dissenters. Be careful, however, that the humor does not become bitter or sarcastic.

Problem 3:

The Family Life Department in a particular diocese sponsors a series of lectures on sex education. One lecture concerns the moral teaching of the Catholic Church. Among other things, the priest giving the lecture tells his audience that in certain situations it is moral and right for a Catholic couple to practice contraception—that acts of masturbation are a natural part of growing up and that such acts can sometimes be justified as the lesser of two evils (since, if the acts of masturbation were not performed, the youth might have an extramarital affair with somebody else)—and that the homosexual condition is not curable and, for that reason, a "loving relationship" between two homosexuals can be accepted as the lesser of two evils (since the "alternative" would be a promiscuous relationship with many homosexuals).

The Family Life Department not only presents these views but insists in response to questions that such opinions are in conformity with the Church's teaching. Accordingly, the following letter is sent to a Cardinal in the Vatican requesting a clarification of the Church's teaching.

Sample Letter to Cardinal Requesting Clarification of Church's Teaching:

Your Eminence,

Enclosed is a transcript from a tape made of a course given on sex education for adults at (*here the writer names the parish and diocese*) last June by Father (*name*), the Associate Diocesan Director of Family Life. While not a member of that particular parish, I have had occasion to listen to the tape and, of course, this particular course is making the rounds of the parishes in our diocese.

Many of us are confused by the contents of this tape/transcript. For instance:

—Is it permissible under extenuating circumstances to practice birth control?

—Is diocesan recognition of the group Dignity encouraged by the Holy See; the appointment of 12 priests to say liturgies for this group; or having Dignity speak to young adults? (They are, by admission, practicing homosexuals.)

—Did Christ suffer concupiscence as presupposed by this transcript?

—Is masturbation truly the lesser of two evils—better than getting a girl pregnant?

—And finally, may I in good conscience teach the contents of this course to my six children? (The reason for this course was to assist parents in teaching their children Catholic morality.)

A good course on Catholic morality is, of course, imperative in this age of amorality and immorality, but I write to ask if the moral issues being taught here are truly the positions taken by the Catholic Church.

Your answer will truly be appreciated.

Respectfully,
(*signature of writer*)

Comment:

This letter, based on one that was actually sent, is an *exceptionally* good approach for four reasons. First, the letter itself is short and compact. Second, the appropriate documentation is included. Third, the letter makes no charges but simply asks questions about the Church's position. Fourth, the letter informs the Vatican of the impact that the lecture series is having on many Catholics.

Problem 4:

The diocesan paper keeps printing columns by those who dissent from Church teaching.

Sample Letter to the Diocesan Bishop Requesting a Meeting:
(Copy to the Vatican)

Your Excellency,

Our diocesan newspaper regularly publishes articles that sharply criticize official Catholic teaching and that even question the activities of the Holy Father. I enclose six articles as samples.

For the life of me, I find it difficult to understand why a diocesan Catholic newspaper would be propagandizing against the Pope.

Please stop such articles and replace them with articles supporting the Pope's views. There are many Catholic writers who are both good journalists and loyal to Catholic Doctrine, but none of them appear regularly in the diocesan newspaper.

I personally know a number of Catholics who have lost their faith in Church teachings because of the articles that have appeared in our diocesan newspaper. I am sure there are many others that I do not know and their number will certainly grow by leaps and bounds if articles by the dissenters continue to appear in the diocesan newspaper and are not counterbalanced by effective articles supporting the Pope.

Would it be possible to have a meeting to discuss this question? It is of such importance to Catholics in our area that I would like to present additional material to you on this subject.

Respectfully yours,
(name)

Comments:

In addition to writing to the bishop—and to the Vatican itself—a letter might be sent to all the priests of the diocese pointing out that the diocesan paper regularly publishes dissent to the Pope but not columns supporting him.

Another possible course of action is to ask Catholics to sign a petition requesting the bishop to permit an orthodox Catholic columnist to appear every week in the paper to respond to attacks on Church doctrine. By such means, public consciousness can be concentrated on the question: "Why does the diocesan paper refuse to allow an effective presentation of the Pope's view?" The more the public becomes aware that such censorship is taking place, the more difficult it is for Church dissenters to continue their policies.

A third way to publicize the repressive policies of the diocesan newspaper is to ask parish councils, Knights of Columbus groups, and other Church societies to pass resolutions requesting that an orthodox columnist appear in the diocesan newspaper. If it is difficult to get existing Church organizations to go on record concerning this matter, ad hoc groups should be formed in as many parishes as possible. Without bitterness, but with persistence, orthodox Catholics must keep on working until the power of the dissenters is checked.

Even if the local bishop himself attacks you for your efforts, do not give up.

I make this last point because I have just read a series of articles in the newspapers on the conflict between the Holy Father and certain bishops in the United States who seem to be sympathetic to the dissenters. While these bishops publicly deny that such a conflict exists, they are outraged because orthodox Catholics have been writing to te Pope expressing concern about what is going on in their dioceses. These bishops are upset because Rome is listening to such letters.

That very fact shows the importance of letter writing!

In the article quoted, the bishops who seem to sympathize with the dissenters tried to discredit the Catholics writing to Rome. They charged that their reports were inaccurate. One bishop branded these loyal Catholics as "fundamentalists" and complained that Rome did not understand that such Catholics should be ignored.

How ironic that this bishop should, on the one hand, call for "openness" and "dialogue" and, on the other hand, dismiss and even sneer at the views of orthodox Catholics who raised questions about the happenings in his diocese! However, I mention the response of this bishop to make loyal Catholics aware that they may in fact have to endure such criticism. This is the reason it is important, if at all possible, to document the statements you are making because a frequent ploy of the dissenters is to deny what is actually happening.

If dissenters or even bishops attack you personally—if they sneer at you as "fundamentalists"—respond calmly but hold your ground. If you establish yourself as likable, those who try to discredit you by personal attacks will themselves end up looking bad.

In any situation where dissent is being promoted by an official Church organization (e.g., a newspaper or religious education program) you might point out that such programs are being financed largely by donations made to the parish or diocese by orthodox Catholics. Using such funds to promote dissent amounts to an unfair trick on orthodox Catholics, who naturally thought that their donations would be used to support the Pope and his teachings—not the views of those who attack him.

If you are in a diocese where the bishop does not sympathize with dissent but is silent because he thinks a public statement would make things worse, then it is important, without attacking the bishop in any way, to make people aware that his silence does not mean his consent because the dissenters will almost certainly claim it does.

WHAT IF OUR EFFORTS SEEM TO BE FRUITLESS?

These sample letters have represented only a few illustrations of many possible situations that orthodox Catholics could encounter. As we work to promote the true teaching of the Church, we will sometimes be encouraged by the progress we are making. At other times, however, our efforts may seem to be utterly useless.

Suppose that you and the other members of your group have written to the Vatican and done everything in your power to correct a real abuse in your diocese with respect to Catholic teaching. Yet nothing happens. Apparently unchecked in any way, the abuse continues. How should such a crisis be faced?

The first step is to check again to make sure that you have in fact done everything possible—in other words, to study and observe if you have acted the way most likely to obtain a favorable response from the Vatican. In this regard, I asked a layman whom I know to have great experience working with the Vatican to present his own thoughts about how Rome usually responds in such situations. I will call this layman Mr. Thomas. Here is his advice to Catholics who write to the Vatican and appeal for help in their local area:

Faithful Catholics should understand that the diocesan bishop is the supreme authority in his diocese; the Holy See will not interfere in matters within a diocese unless it has clear evidence that the bishop is not fulfilling his responsibilities, and that the resulting consequences may be serious for the Church. This means that all matters of injustice, false teaching, or unlawful practice within a diocese must be brought to the attention of the local bishop, and his response or lack of response carefully documented.

Catholics often make the mistake of not communicating with their bishop because they assume it will do no good. However, when they communicate their concerns to the Holy See, the inclination *there* is to simply bring the matter to the local bishop's attention, or to recommend that the concerned do so. The Holy See is swamped with work and will not accept the burden of doing a bishop's work for him.

When faithful Catholics have a legitimate concern about error or abuse in their diocese, therefore, they should carefully document the error or abuse; they should limit themselves as far as possible to the most clear violations of Church law or teaching; they should limit themselves to one issue at a time; they should limit themselves to the smallest amount of documentation needed to make their point; they should document their unsuccessful attempts to resolve the issue at a lower level; and, finally, they should make absolutely sure that they always appear respectful, charitable, and patient, regardless of any provocation they may experience from authorities in the diocese. This documentation should then be sent to their bishop, with a polite, respectful letter requesting help.

If diocesan authorities (including pastors, school principals, teachers, etc.) communicate with them orally, for example by telephone or through a meeting, they should send a letter to the authority involved, expressing what they understood that authority to have said and any difficulties which they may still have. This way the oral statements become a matter of written record.

Faithful Catholics sometimes find themselves unable to communicate with their bishop because he will not respond to their letters. In such a case, they should write to the Apostolic Pro-Nuncio in Washington D.C., and explain the nature of their concern and the fact that they seem unable to reach their bishop. They should ask for the Pro-Nuncio's assistance in bringing their concern to their bishop's attention. They should understand that the Pro-Nuncio is not their bishop's superior, and that he must handle the problem with tact and diplomacy. Any response from the Pro-Nuncio should be read with this understanding. If their bishop does not seem to understand their concern, they might ask the Pro-Nuncio to help them explain the matter better. They should then approach their bishop again about their concern.

If their bishop does not respond to their needs, and this has been carefully documented, members of the faithful have the right to bring the matter to the Holy See. If they do this, they must provide the evidence that their bishop has refused or failed to help them.

Faithful Catholics are welcome to contact groups such as Catholics United for the Faith for advice and guidance. They have many years of experience and a great amount of information in their files which can be helpful to faithful Catholics. They can usually provide documents giving the official teaching or required practice of the Church which loyal Catholics would need in bringing their concerns to higher authority. They can also advise and assist these Catholics in communicating with their bishops, the Apostolic Pro-Nuncio, and, if necessary, with the Holy See.

All correspondence with Church authorities in these matters must be polite, friendly, and patient, regardless of the circumstances. It is important that higher authorities view the faithful Catholics involved as respectful and charitable. A bitter, angry or judgmental attitude when addressing Church authorities, regardless of how justified it may seem, runs a serious risk of being ignored.

Mr. Thomas makes two other important points. First, the Vatican is often active behind the scenes. Therefore, if we do not see anything happening in response to our requests, this does not mean that nothing at all is taking place. From my own experience, I can verify this remark of Mr. Thomas. I know of two instances where the Vatican was most active in bringing about changes in a diocese—yet it was all done quietly and in such a way that the Vatican actions were not known by those whose letters had brought the matter to the attention of Rome in the first place. This is part of the "diplomacy" to which Mr. Thomas refers. Even while making changes, the Vatican will try very hard to avoid embarrassing the local bishop.

Because it can be frustrating for loyal Catholics when they write to Rome and do not see any immediate results from their letters, Mr. Thomas also recommends something that we have stressed throughout these books—the formation of support groups for loyal Catholics. As he puts it:

Many faithful Catholics feel isolated; their faith can be nourished and strengthened by contact with others who follow the Pope and support the Magisterium. Such groups should be social as well as spiritual. Once formed on the basis of mutual need for support, such groups can provide incentives for studying the faith and for appropriate works to promote the faith. Catholic families should actively seek each other out to help establish a Catholic environment for their children.

I thank Mr. Thomas for sharing his experiences with us. If we are to be effective, it is important for us to know about things such as the "Vatican diplomacy". As Mr. Thomas says, the Vatican will usually not respond if a bishop is under public attack, even if the cause is just because such public attacks can seem to be undermining legitimate Church authority. In addition (and this can be a very frustrating situation for Catholics), since the diocesan bishop has been appointed by the Holy Father, he will naturally have the benefit of doubt in any situation where there is no evidence. Thus, it can happen that you and your group know for certain that certain things are going on in the diocese. But the deviations from the faith are flatly denied by local Church authorities and you have no way of proving your statements. In such a situation, it is still helpful to write to Rome because, even though you cannot provide the evidence, you are speaking the truth. If the Vatican believes you—and, in God's Grace, they will—then they will often respond in another way that will improve the situation in your diocese . . . even though, because of the lack of evidence, they may not be able to rule directly on the specific matter that you bring to their attention.

An obvious question might arise at this point. why is the Vatican so careful to act diplomatically? If a local bishop is not doing what the Pope wants, why not simply remove the bishop? From conversations I myself have had, I can say that one reason is Rome's experience in the past and the concern that the Vatican has about the future. I know of one Cardinal who headed an important Congregation in the Vatican. This Cardinal expressed concern that, in the United States, there was a real danger that whole dioceses could be lost the Church. The potentialities for a schism were that serious.

At the time of the Protestant Reformation not only many dioceses but even many countries departed from the Catholic faith. Leading Vatican officials consider this to be a possibility in our time. The "long-range" strategy of the Vatican is to find more and more bishops who will work as hard as they can in their own dioceses for the promotion of Church teaching. It is Rome's hope that in time these bishops will replace those who now either tolerate or (in some cases) actually promote the dissenters who challenge Church teaching.

Now it is legitimate for loyal Catholics to believe that a stronger policy toward bishops who tolerate dissent might work better than the Vatican's present diplomacy policy. After all, as we saw in Book II, it was legitimate for Paul to disagree with Peter on strategy. Not on doctrine and not on authority—but on strategy. Nevertheless, we should understand what the present Vatican strategy is and we should certainly pray and do everything that we can to make it effective.

But suppose you have done all this. And still you are frustrated. You do not know about what is happening behind the scenes. You wonder whether anything is happening at all.

This may be the cross that Jesus and Mary are asking you to bear. To do everything in your power and yet to seem to be defeated. That is the role that our Blessed Lady had to occupy when she stood under the Cross. She seemed to be totally powerless. She could not give her Son a drink of water when He said, "I thirst". Yet we now know that it was at that very moment that she was the most powerful.

Please do everything you can to promote the true Catholic faith. Write to your local bishop and to the Vatican—and keep on writing. But, if everything seems to fail, stay under that cross. Do not give up. If you get angry, you are in a sense leaving the cross. If you say, "What's the use?" and go on to something else, you are also walking away from the cross. If you will stay and keep on working with the love and the zeal of Christ, then you can be confident that, whether you see any results or not, you will be doing what Our Lord wants.

It is my hope that you will be blessed to see your efforts bear fruit. These books have been written to assist you in that regard. But, whatever the outcome, stay by the Cross of Jesus and pray every day to Our Lady for the grace to persevere.

Appendix II.
Fr. Fox's List of Orthodox Catholic Sources

In Book I, we presented a few examples of books and periodicals that Catholics might find helpful.

Rev. Robert J. Fox (in "Hope for the Isolated Catholic"—a pamphlet quoted earlier in this book) presents a more extensive list of orthodox Catholic sources. Among them are the following:

I. Basic Guide Books:

A. The Sacred Scriptures

B. *Vatican Council II: The Conciliar and Post-Conciliar Documents* (Austin Flannery, O.P., edition of conciliar writings - $4.95)

C. *Liturgy of the Hours* - This is the Church's "Divine Office" which is a recommended prayer not only for priests but for all members of the Church. It is also possible to obtain the "Divine Office" in one volume containing the most important parts (in a book called *Christian Prayer*.)

II. Official Church Documents
(Pope, Vatican Congregations, U.S. Bishops)

A. Examples of Papal Documents would be:

1. Pope Paul VI — *His Church (Ecclesiam Suam*, P 17, 25¢), *Mystery of Faith (Mysterium Fidei*, P 18, 25¢), *Priestly Celibacy (Sacredotialis Caelibatus*, P 19, 25¢), and *Devotion to the Blessed Virgin Mary (Marialis Cultus*, P 25, 35¢).

2. Pope John Paul II — *On Catechesis in Our Time (Catechesi Tradendae*, P 28, 60¢), and *On the Worship of the Eucharist (Dominicae Cenae*, P 29, 35¢).

3. In addition — Pope Paul's letters on Holy Thursday concerning the priesthood and the Holy Eucharist.

B. Examples of some important statements by Vatican Congregations would include:

1. Sacred Congregation for the Sacraments and Divine Worship — (*Inaestimabile Donum*, 1980, M7, 25¢) — Official Instructions concerning Worship of the Eucharistic Mystery.

2. Sacred Congregation for the Doctrine of the Faith — (*Mysterium Ecclesiae*, 1973, M2, 25¢) — This document on the Mystery of the Church is a declaration in defense of the Catholic Doctrine on the Church against certain errors of the present day.

3. Sacred Apostolic Penitentiary — (*Enchiridion Indulgentiarum*, 1968, M13, $4.00) — Contains a summary of the Apostolic Constitution, entitled *The Doctrine of Indulgences*, issued on January 1, 1967 by Pope Paul VI.

C. Other important statements:

1. *General Catechetical Directory* (M9, $1.95) — Holy See's prescription for modern Catholic religious catechesis.

2. *National Catechetical Directory* (M10, $4.95) — Official statement on catechesis of the National Conference of Catholic Bishops (entitled "Sharing the Light of the Faith").

D. Devotion to the Mother of God:

1. Documents of Vatican II — Chapter in the *Dogmatic Constitution on the Church* (*Lumen Gentium*).

2. *Behold Your Mother, Woman of Faith* (1973, M14, 75¢) — Pastoral letter approved by the U.S. Bishops.

3. *Marialis Cultus* (available from the U.S.C.C., 1312 Mass. Ave., NW, Wash., DC 20005) — Apostolic exhortation on a true devotion to the Mother of God issued by Pope Paul VI on February 2, 1974.

III. Catholic Newspapers

A. *The Wanderer* — (a subscription includes *Reflections*, a quarterly book review supplement). The Wanderer Press, 201 Ohio Street, St. Paul, MN 55107, phone 1-612-224-5733 ($20.00 per year).

B. *The National Catholic Register* — 6404 Wilshire Blvd., Suite 900, Los Angeles, CA 90025. Toll-free order number: (24 hour service) 1-800-421-3230 or in California 1-213-821-8153.

C. *Catholic Twin Circle* — Same address and phone numbers as *The National Catholic Register*.

D. *L'Osservatore Romano* — Management Office, Vatican City, Italy ($30.00 ordinary mail, $52.00 air mail).

IV. Catholic Magazines

A. *Homiletic and Pastoral Review* — 86 Riverside Drive, New York, NY 10024 ($18.00 per year; $33.00 for two years).

B. *Immaculata* — Knights of the Immaculata, 1600 W. Park Ave., Libertyville, IL 60048.

C. *Soul* — World Apostolate of Fatima (Blue Army), Ave Maria Institute, Washington, NJ 07882 ($2.00 yearly, $5.00 for three years).

D. *Fidelity* — Box 60217, St. Paul, MN 55107 ($15.00 per year).

V. Publications and Distribution Centers

A. *Christendom College Press* — Route 3, Box 87, Front Royal, VA 22630 (Phone 1-703-636-2908).

B. *Catholic Sales, Books and Gifts* — 12525 West Lisbon Road, Brookfield, WI 53005 (Toll-free phone 1-800-558-8637; Wisconsin 1-414-781-0217).

C. *Stella Maris Books* — Box 11483, Fort Worth, TX 76110 (Phone 1-817-924-7221).

D. *Lay Witness* — (Publication of Catholics United for the Faith), CUF, 222 North Ave., Box S, New Rochelle, NY 10801 (Phone 1-914-235-9408).

E. *Trinity Communications* — P.O. Box 3610, Manassas, VA 22110 (Phone 1-703-369-2429).

VI. Youth Programs

A. *Youth Mission for the Immaculata* — (Sponsor ten-day programs) Brother Francis Mary, Franciscan Friars, 1600 West Park Ave., Libertyville, IL 60048.

B. *Cadets of Fatima* — (Youth section of the World Apostolate of Fatima) Study key books which include *Catholic Truth for Youth, Saints and Heroes Speak* and the Marian Catechism. Cadet-Kit available from Sister Mary Celeste, A.M.I., Cadet Cell Program, Ave Maria Institute, Washington, NJ 07882.

VII. Home Study Aids

A. Grades 1-12 — Seton Home Study Program. Has available college preparatory curriculum with four years of religion, as well as history, English, three foreign languages, four years of math, three years of sciences, logic and analytical reading. For further information, write: Seton Home Study, Front Royal, VA 22630.

B. CCD Texts

1. Twelve-year series by the Daughters of St. Paul. Daughters of St. Paul also offers, among other publications, *Religious Education: Its Effects, Its Challenges Today* and a small pamphlet titled, *Structuring a Successful CCD Program, Teenagers and Purity, Teenagers and Going Steady, Teenagers Looking Toward Marriage* —(62 pages, 75¢). The above booklet recorded on three separate cassettes by the same title ($3.50 each). St. Paul Editions, Daughters of St. Paul, 50 St. Paul Avenue, Jamaica Plain, Boston, MA 02130.

2. *Charity, Morality, Sex and Young People* — (Rev. Robert J. Fox) Our Sunday Visitor, Book Dept., Box 920, Huntington, IN 46730. 225 pages. Toll-free phone no. 1-800-348-2440.

VIII. Cassettes on Human Sexuality and Other Subjects
(from Pope Publications, Box 6161, San Rafael, CA 94903)

A. *Christian Youth and Sex Education* ($5.50)

B. *Christian Youth and Education for Marriage* ($5.50)

C. *Young Christians and the Cults*

D. *The Rosary*

E. *The Glorious and Holy Sacrifice of the Mass*

F. *Story Time with Father Fox*

G. *Teenagers and the Ten Commandments*

H. *To Teach as Mary Did at Fatima*

IX. Church History Materials

A. *A Catechism of the Catholic Church—2000 Years of Faith and Tradition.* (Franciscan Herald Press, 1434 West 51st Street, Chicago, IL 60609).

B. *The Catholic Catechism* by Fr. John A. Hardon, S.J. (FH2, 623 pp. PB, $9.95).

C. *Question and Answer Catechism* by Fr. John A. Hardon, S.J. (FH7, 334 pp. PB, $9.95).

D. Father Fox Audio/Video (available from Trinity Communications, P.O. Box 3610, Manassas, VA 22110) — *Instructions in the Catholic Faith* (24 classes averaging 33 minutes each—26 classes of 30 minutes each for video). Audio cassettes: $65.00. Video cassettes on both VHS and Beta-Max: $500.00. An accompanying book covering all the lessons is called *The Catholic Faith* ($7.95). Other individual cassettes by Fr. Fox are available from Trinity at $5.00 apiece: *The Work of the Holy Angels*, *The Catholic Priesthood Today*, *Two Hearts Cassette* (on the Sacred Heart of Jesus and the Immaculate Heart of Mary), *Fatima Is For the World*, *Fatima and Eucharistic Reparation*, and *Father Fox Teaches Grades 1-6*.

E. *Catholic Truth for Youth* — 34 lessons covering all the major tenets
of the Catholic faith (464 pp., Ave Maria Institute, Washington, NJ
07882, $5.75). For inspiration and depth, the youngsters should read
Saints and Heroes Speak (512 pp., $7.50, also Ave Maria Institute).

X. Orthodox Catholic Colleges With No Influence From Church Dissenters

A. Christendom College (Route 3, Box 87, Front Royal, VA 22630;
phone 1-703-636-2908).

B. Thomas Aquinas College (10000 North Ojai Road, Santa Paula, CA
93060).

C. Magdalen College (270 D.W. Highway South, RFD 5, Bedford,
NH 03102).

D. St. Ignatius Institute (University of San Francisco, San Francisco,
CA 94117).

XI. Religious Communities Free From Influence of Church Dissenters

A. Legionaries of Christ (393 Derby Ave., Orange, CT 06477)

B. Oblates of the Virgin Mary (Our Lady of Grace Seminary, 1105
Boylston, Boston, MA 02215)

C. Norbertines (Order of Canons Regular of Premontre, St. Michael's
Seminary, 1042 Star Route, Orange, CA 92667)

XII. Catholic Media: Radio and Television

A. Eternal Word Television Network (5817 Old Leeds Road, Birming-
ham, AL 35210; phone 1-205-956-9537)

B. The Catholic Voice of America (Write: Edgar Debany, 42 Olive
Street, Brooklyn, NY 11209)

XIII. Catholic Organizations

A. Apostolate for Family Consecration (House of St. Joseph, Box 220, Kenosha, WI 53141; phone 1-414-652-6271)

B. CREDO (Box 66601, Houston, TX 77006)

C. Catholics United for the Faith (222 North Avenue, Box S, New Rochelle, NY 10801)

Appendix III.
Further Reflections on What Can Change in Church Teaching

This appendix provides some additional thoughts on a topic considered in Book I where we looked at the attempt of Church dissenters to discredit the teaching of the Church on questions such as contraception (or on any other matter that they wish) by claiming that in other areas the Church has been mistaken and changed Her teaching.

Two common examples used by Church dissenters are the question of usury and the question of religious liberty. Church dissenters will tell you that at one time in Her history the Church taught strongly that it was immoral for lenders of money to charge interest on their loans. Now, however, that teaching has changed and the Church does allow money-lenders to charge a reasonable rate of interest. Therefore, conclude the dissenters, this is an example of a mistake in Church teaching and it "proves" that the Church's teaching on contraception or divorce or any other moral question could also be mistaken.

A similar argument is presented on the question of religious liberty. The dissenters point out that at one time in Her history, the Church insisted strongly on the obligation of the state to promote the true Catholic religion. Now, state the dissenters, Vatican Council II has put forth the position that the state has no such obligation and Vatican Council II has also emphasized that the best situation is one in which the state provides religious liberty for different viewpoints. Therefore, conclude the dissenters, this is one more illustration of erroneous Church teaching—with the Popes at one time emphasizing strongly a moral teaching they have now abandoned.

There are, of course, many other examples that the dissenters attempt to present. The blunt truth is that dissenters throw every possible objection they can at Church teaching in their efforts to undermine the authority and credibility of the Pope. As we pointed out in Book I, one of the most ironic things about this tactic of the dissenters is that they themselves have changed their position so many times that, even if what they say about the official teaching of the Church were true, the dissenters themselves would have committed far more mistakes in their own teaching than they could point to with respect to the Church.

However, that still leaves us with a problem. Is it really true that the Church has made mistakes in the strong teaching She presented in the past on usury and religious liberty? If so, does this indicate that She could be mistaken on questions such as contraception or divorce or pre-marital sex?

WHAT HAS BEEN SAID BEFORE

In this section I will presume what we discussed already in Book I. In that Book, we made a number of important distinctions: the distinction between doctrine and discipline, the distinction between the official teaching of the Church and the Pope expressing his own views, the distinction between the Pope dealing directly with a question and considering it in "obiter dictum" fashion or presuming something that is not taught directly, the distinction between teaching in a final or binding way and teaching in a provisional fashion, and the distinction between the extraordinary magisterium and the ordinary magisterium (with the important truth that the ordinary magisterium can also be infallible under certain circumstances).

On questions where Church dissenters argue that current Church teaching is mistaken (e.g., contraception, divorce, pre-marital sex), we are faced with teaching that is doctrinal, official, dealing directly with a subject, and intended by the Popes to be final and binding. Therefore, when the dissenters talk about "past Church mistakes", the first question to ask is whether one or more of these necessary elements are absent in the "past teaching".

THE GALILEO CASE

To take just one instance, the dissenters sometimes try to discredit the Church by bringing up the question of Galileo. Galileo had challenged the common scientific belief of the day that the sun revolved around the earth. What the dissenters rarely mention, however, is that Galileo had gone beyond a simple scientific finding to challenge the accuracy of the Bible. Galileo had argued that, since the earth revolved around the sun, this proved that the Bible was mistaken.

It was Galileo's contention that Scripture could be in error which provoked a study of his work by eleven theologians representing the Holy Office. In contrast, the scientist Nicholas Copernicus drew no protest from the Holy See when, more than twenty years before Galileo was born, he publicly presented the view that the earth revolved around the sun. Far from condemning Copernicus (as Protestant religious leaders like Martin Luther had done), the secretary of the Holy Office, Cardinal Bellarmine, made this statement: "If ever the Copernican theory be really demonstrated, we must then be more careful in explaining those passages of the Scriptures which appear contrary to it. We must then say that we do not understand their meaning rather than declare a thing false which has been proved true."

There were two important differences between Copernicus and Galileo. First, Copernicus did not insist that the Bible was in error. Second, Copernicus put forth his view as a scientific theory while Galileo taught it as a scientific certainty. Galileo's claim of "certainty" aroused strong opposition from many scientists of his own age (and many scientists of the present age, based upon the findings of Einsteinian relativity, would agree that Galileo was rash and even incorrect in arguing that the evidence available at the time made his view a "certainty" rather than a "theory").

The importance of all this for our study of the Church becomes clear when it is realized that in 1616 the Vatican congregation judging the case forbade Galileo to promulgate his view *as a certainty*. In making this ruling about "certainty", the Vatican congregation was echoing the views of scientists, both of that age and of the present.

Does this mean that the Vatican congregation used correct judgment in its decision about Galileo? Not at all. To the contrary, the theologians who wrote the Vatican decree erred by insisting upon a false interpretation of the Biblical texts under review. However, and this is the crucial point, the Pope of the time, Paul V, refused to sign the decree prepared by the theologians. The Pope made it clear that he did not want the Papacy to become involved in deciding whether the Copernicus-Galileo position was true or untrue. Instead, Pope Paul V wrote to Cardinal di Zoller that

"Holy Mother Church had not condemned the opinion of Copernicus, nor was it condemned as heretical . . . but only as rash".

Galileo had promised to abide by the verdict of 1616. Sixteen years later, after he had broken this promise, a Vatican congregation once again undertook a study of the Galileo case. And again the Pope of the time, Urban VIII, declined to sign the statement of the Vatican congregation, preferring that the Papacy not decide the ultimate truth or falsity of the Copernicus-Galileo theory. In fact, as Galileo lay dying, he received from the Holy Father a personal blessing.

In summary, Church authorities argued that the views put forth by Galileo were simply an unproved scientific hypothesis (which they were at the time), and since his "findings" were being used by some as an excuse to charge that the Bible could be in error, Galileo was told, as a disciplinary matter, not to present his personal opinion as if it were something established by science beyond all doubt. (It should also be remembered that this disciplinary decision was made at a time when Church leaders had not only spiritual authority but a certain temporal authority in view of the relation between Church and state.)

For additional information on the Galileo case, I refer readers to a fine article by Rev. Valentine Long, O.F.M. in June 1981 issue of *Homiletic and Pastoral Review*. (The same author also treats the Galileo case in his 1982 book *Upon This Rock*, published by Franciscan Herald Press.) Since I have used Fr. Long's article as the basis for what I have presented here, I think it is only appropriate to quote directly his words of conclusion. Father Long writes:

> Lovers of the Holy, Catholic, Apostolic Church—like Newman and most assuredly our gloriously reigning John Paul II—would see in the final refusal of the two popes to sign badly worded documents, not an accident, but the sure guidance of the Holy Spirit. Why do not the present malcontents within the same lovable Church share such favorable sentiments? Why do they not learn the facts of the Galileo case instead of spouting off their ignorance of them at the expense of the divinely founded institution they apparently do not love but will not leave? Why, indeed? God knows the answer, whatever it is.

THE KEY DISTINCTION: ABSOLUTE AND RELATIVE

But let us return to the usury and Church-state questions. Is the former Church teaching on usury and the Church-state relationship conceded by the present Church to have been erroneous? If so, does this mean that the Church's teaching on contraception (or other moral questions) might also be erroneous?

In approaching this question, a key distinction must always be kept in mind. It is the distinction between Church teachings that are meant to be absolute and Church teachings that are relative to a particular time and age.

This is a distinction that is almost always ignored by Church dissenters. In trying to discredit the Church's teaching on contraception by pointing to historical examples involving usury and the relation of Church and state, are not the Church dissenters really arguing as follows: "If we can prove that any Church teaching in the past has been changed, this means that any teaching of the present could also be changed. If we can prove that the Church ever made a mistake, this proves that anything the Church says now could also be a mistake."

In other words, the dissenters operate on an "all or nothing" basis. Either everything the Church has always taught remains the same or everything can be changed. Obviously there can well be a middle ground in which some teachings can change and others cannot. This is the distinction to which I am referring when I use the terms "absolute" and "relative" with respect to Church teaching.

Most dissenters appear to operate on the belief that all Church teachings are relative to a particular time and culture. In other words, no matter what the Church may have taught at one historical period, that teaching could be changed.

In defending the Church's infallible teaching against the claims of the dissenters, loyal Catholics emphasize rightly that many Church teachings are unchanging and infallible. It should be noted in this regard that Vatican Council II (the very Council so often falsely used by the dissenters to support their position) emphasizes the unchanging nature of many Church doctrines when it says:

And the Church affirms, too, that underlying all changes there are many things that do not change, and which have their ultimate founda-

tion in Christ who is the same yesterday, today, and forever.
(*Gaudium et Spes*, 10)

However, the fact that loyal Catholics believe that many Church
teachings are absolute does not mean that we believe every Church
teaching is absolute. There are in fact some teachings that are relative to a
particular time and age and such teachings can change in a different time
and age.

Let us give an example of an absolute teaching and a relative teaching.

An absolute teaching would be the following: "The direct killing of an
innocent human being is immoral." This teaching has always been the
doctrine of the Church. It always will be. Although we are permitted to
take the life of an unjust aggressor if this is the only way to defend
ourselves, we can never take the life of an innocent person. This absolute
teaching is true today, will be true tomorrow, and always has been true.

In contrast, what would be an illustration of a relative teaching?

As one example, let us imagine a mother who has two small
children—John and Susan. John is six years old and Susie is four. The
family lives near a very crowded thoroughfare that is often bustling with
traffic. Cars along this thoroughfare consistently reach speeds of sixty
miles an hour.

Conscious of the danger to her two children, there is one teaching that
the mother emphasizes over and over again to John and Susie. Practically
every day she says to them: "You are *never, never, never* to cross that
street unless either I or your father is present to guide you."

This is a most important teaching—as the constant emphasis by the
mother shows. It is a teaching that, if violated by John or Susie, could
easily result in the loss of their lives. Yet it is in fact a relative teaching.
Twenty years from the time that the mother speaks like this to her two
children, will John and Susie still be bound to the teaching never to cross
that street unless their mother or father is present? At that point John will
be twenty-six and Susie will be twenty-four. Of course they will no longer
be bound by the former teaching.

THE LANGUAGE SEEMS ABSOLUTE

But suppose an objector were to say to the twenty-six year old John or the twenty-four year old Susie: "I can quote your mother's exact words of twenty years ago. She said: 'You must *never, never, never* cross the street.' Never means not ever. Therefore, this teaching was meant to be binding even when you are twenty-four and twenty-six. Thus, if you cross the street now, you are admitting that what your parents said in the past was mistaken."

While we would recognize that such an argument is incorrect, it does illustrate an important point. Sometimes a teaching can sound as if it is absolute. Sometimes words like "never" can be used—which literally means "not ever". Nevertheless, even when such words are used, it is not necessarily true that the teaching is meant to apply for all times. If we were to ask the mother of John and Susie, would she not certainly tell us that her teaching was not meant to apply when John was twenty-six and Susie was twenty-four?

Then what was the mother really saying? She was saying that John and Susie should not cross the street unattended because that is much too dangerous an activity for a six year old boy and a four year old girl. Then why didn't she put it that way? Why didn't she say: "Don't cross the street until you develop the proper judgment?" After all, that is what she meant.

She didn't put it that way because, as every mother knows, if she had told her children not to cross the street unless they had the proper judgment they might have erroneously concluded some day that they *did* have the proper judgment when in fact they were in serious danger. The whole reason for the force of the mother's teaching is her conviction that, at this particular moment, it is vitally important that a certain policy be followed, no matter what John and Susie may personally believe they have the ability to do. She wants to drive home this lesson with such force that it will be remembered and followed by John and Susie on those occasions when the parents are not present. So she stresses repeatedly that her children must "*never, never, never*" cross that street—even though she does not mean to imply that, under totally different conditions twenty years later, they must still wait for their parents before they cross.

What we have said about the mother of John and Susie can also be true of Holy Mother the Church.

And, just as with John and Susie, the language used by Holy Mother Church may at times seem to be absolute—even though in fact it is relative to a certain time and age. As Susie's mother can tell her "never, never, never" to cross the street unattended—and still not mean the teaching to apply to totally different circumstances some twenty years later—so the Church can tell Catholics of a particular time that "never, never" should such and such an action be performed and still not mean this teaching to apply to totally different circumstances many centuries later.

Before leaving the example of John and Susie, we might also note one other point. Sometimes a relative teaching may be taught much more strongly than an absolute teaching even though the absolute is in itself far more important. Why? Because the teacher judges that, in the particular circumstances, it is the relative question that poses a real problem for the people being taught.

For example, the mother of John and Susie probably does not stress to them at all the absolute teaching that "one must never kill an innocent person". The reason for this lack of emphasis is that the mother knows there is no danger whatever that her six year old son or her four year old daughter will be in a situation where they are likely to kill the innocent. Because she is convinced that this will not be a problem they will face, she may possibly mention only in passing the obligation not to kill the innocent (or perhaps she may not mention it at all to her young children, intending to present that teaching at a later time). In contrast, she emphasizes again and again the relative teaching of not crossing the street. Is this evidence that the mother believes the relative teaching is more important than the absolute one of not committing murder? No. It simply means that she sees no danger of the absolute teaching being violated at the moment while there is a real danger that the relative teaching will be violated.

All that has been said with respect to the mother of John and Susie may be said with respect to the teaching authority of the Church. At times certain teachings will be emphasized with great force—and still be relative. At times such teachings will be emphasized more strongly than teachings that are absolute, not because the absolute teachings are less important, but because the relative teaching poses a crucial problem at the moment.

NOT ONLY THE CHURCH BUT THE BIBLE

Before proceeding further with the two examples of usury and church-state, it should be pointed out that there is one fact the dissenters usually leave out. If their claim were correct that changes in the Church's doctrine on usury and church-state "prove" that the teachings of past Popes were mistaken, then it would not simply be the Popes who erred but the Bible as well.

For it was not just Popes who condemned the lending of money. The Bible itself condemns money-lending (e.g., Leviticus 25:35-37. "If your brother who is living with you falls on evil days . . . do not take interest from him . . . You are not to lend him money at interest, or give him food to make a profit out of it.") And it was not just Popes who insisted on the obligation of the state to promote the true religion. The Bible also insists on such an obligation. For instance, the Old Testament is very explicit about the obligations of the Jewish state to promote the true religion, while refusing to tolerate any other form of religious worship. If it were true that the teaching of Vatican II on religious liberty amounted to an admission that previous Papal teachings on church and state were erroneous, would it not mean also that Vatican II was admitting that similar teachings on church-state put forth in the Bible as coming from God Himself were also erroneous?

When the question is put this way, we see that there must be some explanation. And the explanation is simply this. Both the teaching about usury and the teaching about church-state were in some respects relative to the particular times in which they were made. When presented in those times, the teaching was not mistaken—just as the instruction given to John and Susie by their mother was not a mistake when John was six and Susie was four.

MORAL TEACHINGS THAT INVOLVE SOMETHING MAN-MADE

Another way of putting all this is that some (by no means all) moral teachings involve something that can change in its function because it is man-made.

For instance, usury involves the use of money within the economy of a society. Both money and the economy in general are things created by man. They are artificial, rather than God-made. Past condemnations of usury operated on an absolute principle (still valid today) that it is wrong to make a profit if one is not contributing something. In the economy of the time (not valid today), the lending of money was not considered to be contributing something.

But a new economic system developed in our society. In this new economic system, money took on a somewhat different function. While the basic principle behind the previous Biblical and Papal teaching on money-lending continued to be correct (namely, that it is wrong to make a profit on something that one has not contributed), it became clear that, under the new economic system, money could in itself be something productive. Therefore, while retaining the general principle, the moral teaching on money-lending began to reflect the new function of money in society.

To put it another way, past moral teaching on usury contained both a general principle (absolute) and a particular fact (relative). These two elements led to a concluding moral judgment that was true.

(1) General Principle — It is immoral to charge people a price unless one has given them something (e.g., a service) that has a value equivalent to the price.

(2) Particular Fact — In our society, the lending of money is not a productive service.

(3) Concluding Moral Judgment — Charging a price for lending money is not moral.

What changed was number (2). Because the function of money within the economy changed, a new situation developed in which it was no longer true to say that the lending of money had to be placed in the category of things which produced nothing. Therefore, a "reasonable" interest could be charged—reasonable here meaning an interest proportionate to the contribution made by the lender.

Unless such an interpretation is made, one must hold that not only past Popes but the Bible is inconsistent with the present moral teaching.

The same distinction should be made with respect to church and state. In our modern western culture, we are accustomed to operate under a system in which there is a separation between church and civil government. In contrast, the problem that the Church faced in the Roman Empire, for instance, was that everyone, including those who ran Rome, thought of church and state as being united in a certain way. That was the reason the Roman emperors became involved in matters of religion.

Therefore, when the Church's former teaching was put forth—and when the Bible teaching was put forth—the state created by men possessed a certain function with respect to religion. In our days, the functions of the state have changed and this is possible because the state, as something created by men, can change in its functions. No longer is the state connected with religion as it was in the past.

(1) General Principle (Absolute) — Because the Church is founded by Jesus Christ, both individual Catholics and Catholic organizations have an obligation to promote the Church.

(2) Particular Fact (Relative) — One of the principal functions of the state is to promote a particular religion.

(3) Concluding Moral Judgment — Therefore, since the state is so closely connected with religion, it has the responsibilities of a Catholic organization and ought to be promoting the Catholic Church.

Once again, it was number (2) that changed. Therefore, the present teaching of the Catholic Church on the church-state relationship should not be considered as a repudiation of the past teaching. (In fact, those who argued for the present teaching at the Second Vatican Council were careful to point out that what they were proposing did not involve a radical reversal of the Church's teaching.) While the past teaching of the Church and the Bible was true at the time it was presented, a particular fact essential to this past teaching has now been altered.

CONTRACEPTION

Now let us apply all this to the question of contraception. Does the fact that the Church's teaching changed on usury and church-state mean that the Church's teaching on contraception can also change? No. Unlike usury (which involves the use of money, a man-made item) or the relationship between church and state (which involves the "state", a man-made association), the question of contraception involves the human body and the sexual act between a man and a woman. This is something that is not created by man—and so its functions cannot be changed by man.

Let us imagine that, in some wild kind of science fiction, the function of the human body changed so that the sexual act no longer had anything to do with the procreation of children. Obviously, if such a change took place, then the Church's teaching on the sexual act would also change because the Church's teaching presumes the particular fact that the sexual act has something to do with the procreation of children. But such a physical change is not going to happen because the sexual act is something that is naturally oriented for the producing of children. Therefore, men and women cannot simply get together one day and decide that the sexual act no longer has anything to do with the procreation of children. This would be like men and women getting together and deciding that from now on the sun will rise in the west instead of in the east. The rising of the sun does not depend upon the opinions of men and the fact that sexual intercourse leads to conception is something that also does not depend on the opinions of men.

But if it did depend on the opinion of men—if it were something created artificially by man—then it would be in the category of usury (money) or religious liberty (the state).

Perhaps an additional example will help to illustrate the distinction I am attempting to present.

The Church's moral teaching on contraception can be summarized as follows:

(1) General Principle (Absolute) — Because one of the essential God-given purposes of the act of intercourse is the procreation of children, it is wrong for couples to perform the marital act while also performing another act (e.g., taking a contraceptive pill or using a contraceptive device) designed to prevent the procreative purpose from coming about.

(2) Particular Fact — The person who uses a contraceptive device or takes a contraceptive pill is intending to prevent conception from coming about.

(3) Concluding Moral Judgment — Therefore, it is immoral to take such a pill or use such a device.

Now let us suppose that, as the years go by, a sudden discovery is made that is not at present known. Let us imagine that what we now call a "contraceptive pill" or "contraceptive device" is found to have a very important effect in preventing cancer. And, for the sake of our example, let us suppose two other things as well. First, there is no other medicine that has the same effectiveness in fighting cancer. Second, this good anti-cancer effect is in no way caused by the bad contraceptive effect of the pill or device.

In such a situation, would it be permissible for Catholics to take such a pill or use such a device—in order to combat cancer?

Yes.

Would this mean that the Church's teaching banning contraception had changed? No. The general principle (No. 1) would remain the same. But, as with usury or religious liberty, a particular fact (No. 2) would have changed. Therefore, a device previously banned because it had only one known effect (contraceptive) would now be permitted to those who were using it because of its newly discovered effect (cancer-combatant).

In summary, the Church's teaching banning contraceptive devices or pills is based not only on a general principle (contraception is wrong) but also on a particular fact (these devices or pills are being used for a contraceptive purpose). Both the Catholic Church and society in general assume the truth of this particular fact. There is not the slightest scientific evidence that contraceptive devices prevent cancer or have any other good purposes and, recognizing this, nobody uses these devices except for the purpose of contraception. Therefore, unlike the Church's teaching banning interest on money-lending, the Church's teaching banning contraceptive devices is not going to change.

I hope that what has been written may throw some light on the attempts by Church dissenters to discredit the Church's teachings. Let me conclude by recalling something else that I mentioned in Book I.

One other important criterion to be used is whether, if the Church's teaching were wrong, it would seriously hurt great numbers of the Catholic laity. If the Church's teaching on usury were wrong (and I have argued here that it was not), how many money-lenders would have gone to hell because they felt compelled to reject this Church teaching? If the Church's teaching on church-state were wrong (and I have argued here that it was not), how many Catholics would have lost their faith because of it?

In contrast, if the Church's teaching on contraception were wrong, such a mistake would adversely affect millions and millions of Catholics. It would amount to the imposition of a cross that Christ Himself did not intend. Our belief in the guidance of the Holy Spirit to His Church should convince us that such a mistake would not be permitted by God.

One final point. In talking about John and Susie, we emphasized that a relative teaching can sometimes be presented in a way that seems absolute. This is another reason we need the judgment of a divinely guided Church authority. Just as Susie's mother could tell us whether a teaching presented in seeming absolute words was meant to be applied to her children twenty years later, so the Church's magisterium is the only one that can tell us authoritatively whether a teaching listing terms that might appear at first glance to be absolute was actually relative to a time and age—or, in contrast, meant to apply for all time. With respect to usury and church-state, the Catholic Church has told us that these teachings were not meant to apply to all times. With respect to contraception, the Catholic Church has made the opposite declaration—stressing that Her teaching is just as valid today as it always was and rooting this teaching in the very purposes of the marital act created by God Himself.

Appendix IV.
Reviewing The Book

Here are some questions that summarize Book III. They can be used as a study guide for any groups that wish to discuss the key ideas in the book. They also provide a quick way to review the contents of the book without reading it over again from cover to cover.

I have composed these questions because of my own experience in reading. After I finish a book, I have often discovered that I soon forget many of the principal ideas, although a general impression about the book remains with me.

To remember the main themes of a book, I have found it helpful to compose a few questions that cover the basic ideas of each chapter. I then write down a short answer to each question, and this leaves me with a concise summary of the book's contents that I can read through in five or ten minutes.

Since this method has helped me to remember books, I thought it might be of assistance to others as well. In the pages that follow, therefore, the reader will find a list of questions that summarize this book.

BOOK III

Chapter 1 - *Yes, You Can*

1) Catholics often believe that they can do relatively little to promote orthodox Church teaching unless they have special intellectual ability or other talents. What is the basic reason that such a view is mistaken?
2) Is it easy or difficult for Catholic parents to teach Church doctrine to their children? Does the typical parent really have the time to do this properly?
3) What two general qualities are needed to speak out effectively for orthodox teaching?
4) Under what circumstances does Our Lord Himself advise us to "be a nuisance"?

Chapter 2 - *Strengthening Your Own Faith and The Faith of Your Family*

1) What are the ten points in the spiritual program recommended by Fr. Fox?
2) "Our personal spiritual program should consist of a healthy balance between doctrinal works and devotional works." Why and how?
3) Where can orthodox Catholics find good doctrinal and devotional works?

Chapter 3 - *How a Catholic Home Life Can Overcome Outside Pressures*

1) What are your children likely to encounter in many Catholic schools and religious education programs?
2) Using the Right to Life movement as an example, illustrate how a strong home environment can neutralize the influence of the dissenters.
3) What is a "lived value" and how can we develop such lived values in our home life?

Chapter 4 - *Working Within the Church Community At Large*

1) When we speak of promoting the Church's teaching: a. what are we about, b. what are we not about, c. what could we be about (but always secondary to the essentials of Church doctrine)?
2) Because there is so much dissent around us, we may constantly have to resist a certain temptation. What is it?
3) How can groups of orthodox Catholics solve the following apparent dilemma: "If we fail to speak out on questions of Church discipline, we will not be contributing to some of the most important decisions that today's Church must make. But, if we do speak out on questions of Church discipline, we may not be able to work with other orthodox Catholics who agree fully with us on doctrine but not on certain proposed changes in the Church's discipline."
4) Why must all Catholics be informed as to the key distinction between doctrinal dissent and policy dissent?

Chapter 5 - *Forming An Effective Group to Promote Church Teaching*

1) What are the seven qualities that an effective group should possess?
2) List three advantages that a small group often has over a large group.

3) How might the meetings of the group be structured?

4) What two kinds of Catholics is the group attempting to reach?

5) "There is a sense in which those who are not already convinced cannot be in your group. Yet there is another sense in which they ought to be." Explain.

6) What steps can orthodox groups take in order to multiply their numbers each year?

7) From the activity of the Jehovah's Witnesses, we can learn two things. They are _____.

8) What do studies reveal about the way people are influenced and how does this apply to groups of orthodox Catholics?

9) Using another example from the pro-life movement, illustrate the basic reason that local activity is vital.

10) Give six examples of specific projects that could be undertaken by groups seeking to promote orthodox teaching.

Conclusion

What is the main theme of this book (as well as the two that preceded it)?

The publication of this book was made possible in part through the support of the Christendom Publishing Group. Members are listed below:

Mr. Juan Alvarez
Miss Audrey Amerski
Mrs. Sophie Andrzejewski
Mrs. Mary Ann Armet
Rev. Edward P. Atzert
Rev. Phillip B. Avila-Oliver
Rev. Louis P. Barcelo
Mr. Daniel J. Bauer
LCDR. C. W. Baumann
Mr. & Mrs. James W. Beeson
Mr. & Mrs. Michael D. Belland
Mr. Patrick F. Beno
Mr. Joseph C. Berzanskis
Mr. Raymond Bodine
Mr. Douglas Boyes
Mr. Hugh J. Bradley
Mr. Ronald Branas
Rev. Nicholas Brennan
Mrs. Iona M. Brink
Mr. Kyle C. Brown
Mr. James G. Bruen
Deacon Patrick Bruen
Mr. Paul A. Busam
Mrs. Marie Butkus
Rev. Gerald F. Chapman
Mr. & Mrs. Joseph Chesanek
Christian Life & Truth
Rev. Patrick Clancy
Mrs. Mark Clarke
Mrs. S. J. Conner
Mr. & Mrs. Joseph Connolly
Mr. John W. W. Cooper
Rev. Henry Cosgrove
CH (LTC) Alfred M. Croke
Mr. & Mrs. Chris N. Cuddeback
Mrs. Lynn Custer
Mrs. Ellen L. Dalby
Mr. & Mrs. William A. Dateno
Mr. Americo A. Deacutis
Mrs. Jack Deardurff
Mr. Phil DeFilippo

Rev. Robert J. Dempsey
Mr. & Mrs. Joseph DeStefano
Mr. Carmine D. Diorio
Rev. Daniel B. Dixon
Maj. & Mrs. George S. Dodge
Mr. Jacques Dolbec
Dominican Monastery
   of St. Jude
Mr. & Mrs. Leon W. Doty
Mr. & Mrs. Thomas J. Dowdall
Mr. Gordon H. Dozier
Rev. Edouard J. Duval
Mr. D. N. Ehart
Sr. Ellen (Walton, KY)
Mr. William W. Elliott
Mrs. Betty Emilio
Rev. George S. Endal
Mrs. Ann Erwin
Mr. Edward R. Ettner
Mr. R. G. Faith
Fathers of Mercy
Maj. L. Fecteau
Mrs. Julia Fendryk
Rev. Charles R. Fink
Mr. John A. Finnegan
Mr. & Mrs. James G. Fischer
Mrs. Margaret E. Fitzgerald
Mr. John F. Foell
Mr. & Mrs. J. P. Frank
Miss Clare C. Fredette
Mr. Michael J. Freiling
Mrs. Adele Fricke
Mrs. Virginia Gagnon
Mr. & Mrs. Joseph Garvey
Mrs. Grace M. Gaylord
Mr. Richard Gerhards
Mr. Richard P. Godek
Mr. Carl J. Graham
Dr. & Mrs. Edward Green
Mr. & Mrs. George E. Guettler
Mr. P. Guinan

Mr. Robert E. Hanna
Rev. William M. Hart
Mr. & Mrs. Frank E. Hauck
Mr. David Havlicek
Rev. Brian J. Hawker
Dr. & Mrs. Harold W. Held
Mrs. William Herbert
Mr. Ronald H. Herrmann
Rev. John J. Hilkert
Rev. E. D. Hoffman
Mrs. Edgar Hull
Mr. & Mrs. Philip Humbert
Mr. David Jaszkowiak
Mr. Albert K. Johnson
Mr. Bruce Jones
Miss Kathleen C. Jones
Mr. Edward E. Judge
Mr. & Mrs. Albert Kais
Mr. John S. Kelly
Mr. Edward J. Kenna
Mrs. Jennie E. Kennett
Mrs. Ruth L. Kish
Mrs. Frank Knoell
Mr. Larry G. Krupp
Mr. Frank W. Kullman
Mrs. Michael E. Law
Miss Therese Lawrence
Mrs. Barbara Lekas
Mrs. Theresa Leone
Mr. Leonard L. Letoto
Rev. Harold J. Lewis
Mr. Henry Lopez
Very Rev. Victor O. Lorenz
Mr. William J. Lucas
Mrs. Jackie Luebbert
Mr. & Mrs. William L. MacDonald
Mr. Leo N. Macht
Mrs. Rose M. Madigan
Rev. Thomas V. Manning
Mr. Steven Manwiller
Mrs. Mia Marintez-Myers
Mr. & Mrs. John W. Marshall
Miss Jeanette Maschmann
Mr. Michael J. Matochik
Mr. John A. McCarty
Mr. J. L. McCarty
Mr. Joseph D. McDaid

Mr. & Mrs. Dennis P. McEneany
Mrs. Winifred C. McManamen
Dr. Peter C. Mendes
Rev. Robert A. Meng
Dr. & Mrs. Patrick A. Metress
Mr. Philip L. Metschan
Mr. & Mrs. Larry Miggins
Pam Mock
Rev. Hugh Monmonier
Mr. James B. Mooney
Mrs. Gertrude G. Moore
Mr. Robert E. Morey
Rev. William G. Most
Mr. Leo Mount
Mr. Nicholas J. Mulhall
Mr. N. P. Murphy
Miss Rita Murphy
Mr. Paul O'Connell
Rev. Thomas F. O'Connor
Lt. Col. Michael J. O'Hara
Miss Veronica M. Oravec
Mrs. John F. Parker
Mr. Patrick M. Patin
Rev. Angelo J. Patti
Br. Stephen F. Paul
Mr. Alfred H. Pekarek
Mr. Robert N. Pelaez
Mr. David M. Perkins
Mr. Thomas P. Petersen
Mr. & Mrs. Gerald R. Pfeiffer
Mr. & Mrs. Patrick Pollock
Mr. & Mrs. William H. Power
Mr. Thomas J. Quinn
Mr. Samuel J. Ramirez
Mr. & Mrs. Joseph E. Rau
Rev. Robert A. Reed
Mrs. John Reid
Mr. & Mrs. John J. Reuter
Mr. & Mrs. Michael Roby
Mr. Peter Rocha
Mr. M. V. Rock
Br. Philip Romano
Mrs. Michele Romito
Mrs. Paul Rosenberger
Mrs. Ted Rowell
Miss Agnes J. Ryan
Rev. Ray Ryland

Mrs. Mary Anne Sansone
Mr. Richard W. Sassman
Rev. John D. Sauter
Mr. Edward F. Scanlon
Mr. & Mrs. George Scanlon
Miss Marian C. Schatzman
Miss Constance M. Scheetz
Mrs. Margaret M. Scheetz
Mr. Peter Scheetz
Mrs. Francis R. Schirra
Mr. Ralph Schutzman
Mrs. Richard Schwader
Mrs. Anne S. Scrivener
Dr. John B. Shea
Mr. John R. Sheehan
Miss Anne Sherman
Mrs. Bernice Simon
Mr. G. S. Sims
Dr. Arthur C. Sippo
Rev. Urban J. Snyder
Mr. & Mrs. Raymond Sommers
Mr. & Mrs. James Spargo
Mr. Dan Staniskis
Mr. Elmore W. Steffen

Mr. John S. Steffen
Miss Sylvia H. Stokes
Mr. Michael Sullivan
Mr. John J. Summe
Mr. Leon Suprenant
Mr. Edward S. Szymanski
Mr. Dominic Torlone
Rev. Christopher T. Twohig
Mr. Jerome A. Urbik
Mr. & Mrs. Albert Vallone
Mrs. Alice M. Vandenberg
Dr. John W. Vincent
Mr. William C. Vinet
Mrs. Catherine M. Wahlmeier
Mr. Fulton J. Waterloo
Mr. James F. Waters
Mr. Frank Weiler
Mrs. Helen M. Weir
Mr. Leonard N. Weydert
Mrs. Moody Wharam
Mr. Robert S. Wilson
Mr. Michael C. Winn
Mrs. Marguerite A. Wright
Mr. Steven M. Zarowny